EVALUATION
FOR EDUCATION
& PSYCHOLOGY

This book is dedicated to the ones I love:
John C. Beck and, of course, Ingrid and Anja.

EVALUATION FOR EDUCATION & PSYCHOLOGY

ARLENE FINK

SAGE Publications
International Educational and Professional Publisher
Thousand Oaks   London   New Delhi

For information address:

SAGE Publications, Inc.
2455 Teller Road
Thousand Oaks, California 91320

SAGE Publications Ltd.
6 Bonhill Street
London EC2A 4PU
United Kingdom

SAGE Publications India Pvt. Ltd.
M-32 Market
Greater Kailash I
New Delhi 110 048 India

Printed in the United States of America

Library of Congress Cataloging-in-Publication Data

Fink, Arlene.
    Evaluation for education and psychology / Arlene Fink.
        p.   cm.
    Includes bibliographical references and index.
    ISBN 0-8039-5854-4
    1. Educational evaluation—Methodology.   2. Psychometrics.
    I. Title.
    LB2822.75.F55   1995
    379.1′54—dc20   94-23539

95 96 97 98 99 10 9 8 7 6 5 4 3 2 1

Sage Project Editor: Susan McElroy

Contents

Preface

During the past decade, education program evaluation has made important contributions to teaching, learning, counseling, and testing. This book explains the evaluator's goals and methods in order to provide its readers with the skills they need to review and participate in program evaluations.

The book has nine chapters. They are specifically organized to facilitate learning and are characterized by providing:

an overview of all topics to be covered

learning objectives

textual material

examples of all major concepts (set off in boxes)

separate guidelines for conducting key evaluation activities

forms to use in completing evaluation tasks

checklists of do's and don'ts

summary of the main ideas and topics covered in each chapter

exercises

answers to the exercises

suggested readings

The book also provides readers with a special scoring guide for reviewing the quality of their own and others' evaluations.

The book's chapters are organized according to the main tasks involved in conducting an evaluation:

posing evaluation questions

setting standards of effectiveness

designing the evaluation

sampling participants

selecting information sources

ensuring reliable and valid measurement

analyzing data

reporting the results in written and oral form

planning, managing, and budgeting

Among the special topics covered are:

the use of expert panels to set standards of program effectiveness

how to evaluate the literature of program evaluation

qualitative evaluation methods, including participatory evaluations

evaluation questions

cost-benefit and cost-effectiveness

data management

confidence intervals

statistical and practical significance

reading computer printouts

meta-analysis

oral presentations (slides and transparencies)

budgets

time and task analyses

This book is recommended for program evaluators in education and psychology and for students and faculty in courses with content or topics in education, psychology, sociology, public policy, and anthropology. It can be used by education and counseling program planners and administrators and funders of programs in education and psychology. The book is designed to cover the field and respect the needs of students in education and psychology, as well as those of teachers, counselors, experts in curriculum and instruction, testing specialists, and anyone else interested in understanding and improving teaching and learning.

The examples are taken from programs that include students in all grades and adult vocational and continuing education. They include younger and older students and cover the costs and quality of education, as well as issues as diverse as programs to improve reading and math skills, counsel families at risk for violence, and improve the knowledge, behavior, and self-confidence of teens.

The book includes a running example derived from a high school program to evaluate the effectiveness of a teacher-delivered curriculum in improving high school students' knowledge, beliefs, and self-efficacy in connection with acquired immunodeficiency syndrome (AIDS).[1]

Note

1. Walter, H. J., & Vaughan, R. D. (1993). AIDS risk reduction among a multiethnic sample of urban high school students. *Journal of the American Medical Association, 270,* 725-730.

Purpose of This Chapter

The goal of this text is to provide you with the tools and skills you need to be a perceptive participant in and consumer of program evaluations. This chapter defines evaluation and discusses its purposes and methods.

Program Evaluation

A PRELUDE

A Reader's Guide to Chapter 1

What Is Program Evaluation?

How to Evaluate: The Methods

The Program or Intervention:
Merits, objectives and activities, outcomes, impact, and expenses and costs

Users and Doers of Evaluations

The Composition of Program Evaluation:
Posing questions, setting standards, designing the study, selecting participants, collecting information, analyzing data, and reporting the results

Baseline Data, Interim Data, and Formative Evaluation

Process Evaluation

Qualitative Evaluation

Participatory Evaluation

Evaluation Research, Program Development, and Policy Formation

What Is Program Evaluation?

Evaluation is a diligent investigation of a program's charac-teristics and merits. Its purpose is to provide information on the effectiveness of projects so as to optimize the outcomes, efficiency, and quality. Evaluations achieve this purpose by enabling you to analyze a program's structure, activities, and organization and to examine its political and social environment. Evaluations can be used also to appraise the achievement of a project's goals and objectives and the extent of its impact and costs.

How to Evaluate: The Methods

Evaluations are conducted by using many of the same methods that social investigators rely on to gather reliable and valid evidence. These consist of formulating study questions, setting standards for establishing a program's merits, designing the evaluation, collecting data, and analyzing, interpreting, and reporting the results. Program evaluations require diligence in the choice and application of methods.

The Program or Intervention

At the core of an evaluation is an experimental project or **program,** sometimes called an **intervention.** Programs are system-atic efforts to achieve preplanned purposes, such as advancing knowledge and favorably affecting behavior, attitudes, and practice. Programs may be relatively small (e.g., family support sessions at a single school, a work-study program for seniors in all high schools, a campaign to vaccinate all children in a school district) or relatively large (e.g., Head Start, the Job Corps). Programs can take place in differing geographic and political settings, and they vary in their purposes, structure, organization, and participants.

PROGRAM MERITS

A major evaluation responsibility is to judge a program's merits. A meritorious program has worthy goals, achieves its standards of effectiveness, provides benefits to its participants, fully informs its participants of the potential risks of participation, and does no planned harm. Identifying convincing evidence of program merit, measuring merit, and describing the aspects of the program that are most meritorious often distinguish evaluation from other types of research in education, psychology, and social welfare.

PROGRAM OBJECTIVES AND ACTIVITIES

A program's **objectives** are its planned purposes—for example, to optimize the efficiency of education. A primary function of program evaluation is to provide data on the extent to which a program's objectives are achieved. When assistance is needed in clarifying objectives or in establishing priorities among them, an evaluator might be called on to conduct a needs assessment. A needs assessment was conducted, for example, when the director of curriculum and instruction asked a team of evaluators to conduct a survey of the adequacy of a district's textbooks. Teachers, students, parents, school administrators, and members of the community participated in the survey. The survey found that changing instructional styles, growing emphasis on a diversity of opinions, and a dislike of textbooks necessitated a search for children's literature and historical novels to be used as alternatives to standard texts.

Evaluations also answer questions about a program's activities and offer insight into a program's implementation and management. When an evaluation focuses on the program's activities, it is termed a **process evaluation.** Process evaluations are important in helping develop insights or form hypotheses for later testing on the reasons for the achievement (or lack of achievement) of the program's objectives. Suppose, for example, an evaluation found no differences between two programs to improve the use of seat belts among teen drivers. A wary evaluator would make certain to measure the extent to which each program was implemented according to its prespecified plan. Among the questions the evaluator could ask are: Did all eligible teens participate in each program? Did teachers follow the same instructional plan? Were some teachers simply better than others? Was attendance in both programs similar and similarly enforced?

PROGRAM OUTCOMES

The ultimate, hoped-for outcomes of programs in education, psychology, and social welfare include knowledgeable and compassionate individuals who function effectively in a democratic society. These outcomes are often extremely difficult to evaluate because of lack of consensus over their definition and the time needed to accurately observe them. As a result, many evaluations focus on investigating the extent to which programs achieve more accessible goals and objectives. These include advances in knowledge and favorable changes in values, attitudes, skills, and behaviors. The idea is that if programs can foster the achievement of these objectives, achievement of the more remote outcomes is probable.

PROGRAM IMPACT

Evaluations can research a program's **impact**—that is, the scope of its effects, the duration of its outcomes, and the extent of its influence in other settings and among different people. For example, consider an evaluation of two programs to improve reading ability. Evaluation A concluded that Program A improved reading and that the gains were sustained for at least 3 years; moreover, when Program A was tried out in the schools in another county, students in that county uniformly improved. Evaluation B concluded that participants in Program B also sustained improved reading for 3 years but for fewer people; when the program was tested in another county's schools, the evaluators noted few gains. The evaluators of Programs A and B agreed that Program A had greater impact because its benefits reached more people over a longer period of time.

PROGRAM EXPENSES AND COSTS

Evaluations are concerned with the costs of programs and their relationship to effects and benefits. Typical questions about costs are: How efficiently is the program, school, and district run? What are the costs to the district of adding a required physical education program? If a required physical education program is introduced, which of the following benefits can we expect: fewer days absent, less use of the health care system? For every dollar spent on a physical education program, how much gain in monetary terms can be expected from reduced use of health services and additional funds given to the district by the state because of increased attendance?

Users and Doers of Evaluations

Information from evaluations is used by at least five groups:

1. federal, state, and local government (e.g., a city, county, or state department of education, the National Institute of Education)
2. program developers (e.g., the curriculum department or division in a school or district, the social services departments in cities and counties)
3. policymakers (e.g., a subcommittee on education and human services of the state or federal legislature, the people who make decisions regarding school funding)
4. program funders (e.g., the Office of Education, philanthropic foundations)
5. education and other social researchers (in government, business, public agencies, and universities)

Evaluations sometimes are conducted by teams of individuals, each of whom contributes expertise. Consider the evaluations described in Example 1.1:

Example 1.1. Program Evaluation as an Interdisciplinary Discipline

- A 3-year evaluation of an in-home special education program depended on a team of two professional evaluators, a physical therapist, two special education experts, and a survey researcher. Consultants included a nurse, an economist, and trained data collectors.
- A 3-year evaluation of a 35-project program to improve access to and use of prenatal care by teens relied on a professional evaluator, a case manager, a "mentor," and an economist.
- An evaluation of a national program to train teachers to work in rural and underserved areas relied on three evaluators, three teachers, six members of the communities affected by the program, six parents, and ten students.

The Composition of Program Evaluation

Program evaluations typically consist of the following activities:

1. posing questions about the program
2. setting standards of effectiveness
3. designing the evaluation and selecting participants
4. collecting information
5. analyzing data
6. reporting the results

1. POSING EVALUATION QUESTIONS

The combined answers to evaluation questions are a primary basis for judging a program's merits. Typical evaluation questions are:

- To what extent did the program achieve its goals and objectives?

- What are the characteristics of the individuals and groups who participated in the program?
- For which individuals or groups was the program most effective?
- How enduring were the effects?
- Which features (e.g., activities, settings, management strategies) of the program were most effective?
- How applicable are the program's objectives and activities to other participants in other settings?
- What are the relationships between the costs of the program and its effects?
- To what extent did changes in social, political, and financial circumstances influence the program's support and outcomes?

2. SETTING STANDARDS OF EFFECTIVENESS

Setting standards means deciding on the information needed to provide convincing evidence of a program's effectiveness, an important component of an evaluator's appraisal of merit. For example, consider these possible standards for the objective "to improve children's dietary and other health habits":

- testimony from children (parents, teachers) in the program that children's habits had improved
- observations by the evaluator of improved health habits (e.g., through studies of choices of snacks during and between meals)
- physical examinations by a nurse practitioner revealing evidence of children's improved health status
- a difference in habits and health status favoring children who are in the program over children who are not

The challenge to the evaluator is to identify standards that are appropriate for the program, possible to measure, and credible.

3. DESIGNING THE EVALUATION
AND SELECTING PARTICIPANTS

Evaluation design refers to the way the environment is structured so that any documented effects that seem like results of the program can be linked conclusively to it. Standard evaluation designs include comparing one group's performance over time and comparing two groups at one or many times. For example, suppose five universities plan to participate in an evaluation of a new program to teach the basic principles of evaluation research to its School Corps trainees. The evaluators will have to decide on such issues as whether some or all universities should receive the program, how many times School Corps trainees should be tested to determine the extent of learning, and when they should be tested (before and after each lesson? before and after the program? how long after the program?).

Among the general questions asked by evaluators when considering the design of their study are:

- How many measurements should be made?
- When should the measurements be made?
- How many institutions, groups, or persons should be included in the evaluation?
- How should the institutions, groups, or persons be chosen?

4. COLLECTING INFORMATION

The collection of evaluation information is really a set of tasks that include:

- identifying the variables to measure (e.g., the specific knowledge, performance, attitudes, and behaviors that are the focus of the program's objectives)
- selecting, adapting, or creating measures
- demonstrating the reliability (consistency) and validity (accuracy) of the measures

♦ administering the measures
♦ scoring the measures

Some common sources of evaluation data are:

♦ record reviews
♦ self-administered survey questionnaires
♦ interviews
♦ achievement tests
♦ observations
♦ the published and unpublished literature

5. ANALYZING DATA

The choice of which method of analysis to use is dependent on considerations such as these:

♦ the characteristics of the evaluation question and standards (Do they ask about differences or associations over time among groups? costs and effects? use of services?)
♦ how the variables are expressed: nominally or categorically (did or did not participate in the program); ordinally (Grades 1, 2, 3, 4, etc.); or numerically (scores that range from 1 to 100 on an achievement test)
♦ the number of measures
♦ the reliability and validity of the data

6. REPORTING THE RESULTS

An evaluation report consists of descriptions of a program's characteristics and explanations, and judgments of its merits. The report describes the purposes of the evaluation, presents the methods (including the standard-setting process, research design, sampling, data collection, and analysis) and results, and discusses the program and the implications of the results. Evaluation reports may be oral or written as books, monographs, or articles.

Baseline Data, Interim Data, and Formative Evaluation

Evaluations are conducted to determine the extent to which an intervention or program is effective and efficient in influencing the outcomes of learning and the organization and quality of programs. The evaluator typically assumes that the program is needed and that a program protocol has been prepared to meet the needs. If the assumptions are erroneous and the evaluation continues, the results necessarily will be invalid.

The need for the program is demonstrated by collecting data to show that the participants start out with one or more difficulties in need of an intervention. These baseline data provide facts regarding the participants' condition before the program. Interim data, collected during the course of the program, provide information on the program's progress in meeting the needs of the participants.

Baseline Data. Baseline data are collected before the start of the program to describe the current status. They are used to monitor changes in status and to help explain later findings.

Suppose you are evaluating a reading program. Baseline data can be collected to provide information on the numbers and characteristics of all program participants, including teachers, students, schools, and parents. This information can include teachers' experience, students' achievement scores on standardized reading and other tests, and parents' income and education. Baseline information also can be collected on current attitudes, values, and opinions.

Example 1.2 illustrates some of the reasons program evaluators collect baseline data.

Interim Data or Formative Evaluation. Interim data (sometimes called "formative evaluation") are reported after the start of a program but before its conclusion—say, 18 months after the beginning of a 3-year intervention. Their purposes are to describe the progress of the program and of the evaluation.

Because interim data are always preliminary, they must always be interpreted cautiously. Example 1.3 is an illustration of the need for taking care in interpreting preliminary, formative findings.

Example 1.2. Baseline Data and Program Evaluation

Social Opportunities for Schools (SOS) is a private, nonprofit agency hired to experiment with managing five city schools. SOS commissioned an independent evaluation of the impact of its new management policies on teacher performance, opportunities for parental involvement, program of instruction, principal performance, amount children learned, and school discipline. Before the evaluators begin the formal process of evaluation, they plan on collecting information that answers questions such questions as these:

1. What is the current level of teacher performance?
2. What opportunities are presently available for parental involvement?
3. What courses, learning experiences, and materials make up the curriculum in elementary, intermediate, and high schools?
4. How effective is the principal in dealing with local and state authorities? with parents? with students?
5. What are current student achievement levels?
6. What types of discipline problems does each school have? How are the problems handled? How effectively?

Example 1.3. Formative Evaluation and Interim Data: Proceed With Care

A formative evaluation was conducted 18 months into a 5-year evaluation of the effectiveness of new management policies implemented in five schools by SOS. The evaluation found improvements in teacher and principal performance and increased opportunities for parental participation. At two schools, achievement scores in reading and science improved significantly. The evaluators concluded that the formative results suggested SOS was showing great promise in all five schools.

At the end of 5 years, the evaluators were forced to modify their conclusions. Only one school maintained its improved student performance in science. Several of the highest rated teachers had quit in each of the five schools, citing the management policies as a main reason. At all five schools, parent participation was at an all-time high, and the curriculum had been revamped for the better. The evaluators suggested that the early benefits may have been the result of excitement at participation in a new program. They concluded that SOS had reaped some benefits but that the program needed substantial revision if it were to achieve its objectives.

Accordingly, although formative evaluations and interim data sometimes may appear to be useful, they also may be misleading; further, they are extremely expensive to collect. With relatively short programs—say, 2 years or less—they are probably not very useful at all. Some evaluators will not participate in studies of interventions that are not carefully defined and standardized (and therefore not in need of formative evaluation), suggesting that such analyses belong to the program developers. Consider Example 1.4.

Example 1.4. Questions Asked in a Formative Evaluation of a Program for Critically Ill Children

Many experts agree that the emergency medical services needed by critically ill and injured children differ in important ways from those needed by adults. As a result, a number of states have attempted to reorganize their emergency services to better care for children. One state commissioned a 3-year evaluation of its program. It was concerned specifically with the characteristics and effectiveness of its about-to-be implemented intervention to improve transfers from adult inpatient or intensive care units and to maximize quality of care for children with cardiopulmonary arrest in the emergency department and in intensive care units.

In planning the evaluation, the evaluators decided to check a sample of medical records in 15 of the state's 56 counties to determine whether sufficient information was available to use the records as a main source of data. Also, the evaluators planned to release preliminary findings after 12 months. This preliminary report would involve reviews of records and interviews with physicians, hospital administrators, paramedics, and families. An expert's review of the evaluation raised these questions:

1. Although the evaluation is a "3-year evaluation," does that mean 3 years of data collection? How much time will you need to plan the evaluation?

2. Interim data have been promised in a year. Can you develop and validate medical record review forms in time to collect enough information to present meaningful findings?

3. Can you develop, validate, and administer the survey forms in the time available?

4. To what extent will the interim and preliminary analysis answer the same or similar questions? If they are very different, will you have sufficient time and money to do both well?

5. Will a written or an oral interim report be required?

Process Evaluation

A **process evaluation** is concerned with the extent to which planned activities are executed, and its findings may be reported at any time. Process evaluations are nearly always useful. In a randomized trial of three programs to improve school attendance rates among the chronically truant, for example, a process evaluation concluded that implementation of each program was less than perfect and thus introduced a conservative bias into the results of the outcome evaluation. Consider Example 1.5:

Example 1.5. Process Evaluation:
Interventions to Improve Attendance Rates

Three approaches to the reduction of truancy were tried. The first program emphasized "truancy prevention," with students sent to truancy centers offering counseling by social service workers and other family services. The second program relied on the police to pick up, search, and handcuff truants before taking them to truancy centers. The third program relied on education and counseling led by former truants. During the course of the 2-year evaluation, all chronically truant students were to be surveyed at least once regarding their involvement in their assigned program and the extent to which they understood its purposes and adhered to its requirements. Face-to-face interviews after 18 months revealed that 74 of 100 students (74%) in the prevention program actually had participated in the full program; 111 (63%) had fully participated in the second; and 32 of 101 (about 32%) had been involved in the third. These findings helped explain the apparent failure of the third intervention to achieve positive results when compared with the other two.

Qualitative Evaluation

Qualitative evaluations collect data from in-person interviews, direct observations, and written documents (e.g., private diaries). These evaluations aim to provide personalized information on the dynamics of a program and on participants' perceptions of their outcomes and impact. Qualitative evaluation methods are useful for a program the goals of which are in the process of being defined and to test the workability of the evaluation's methods. Because they are "personalized," qualitative methods may add emotion and tone to purely statistical findings and provide a means of gauging outcomes when reliable and valid measures of those outcomes are unlikely to become available in time for the evaluation report.

Qualitative methods are employed in program evaluations to complement the usual sources of data (e.g., standardized surveys, achievement tests). Example 1.6 illustrates some of the uses of qualitative information in program evaluation.

Example 1.6. Uses of Qualitative Methods in Program Evaluation

1. To evaluate the effectiveness of a campaign to get heroin addicts to clean their needles with bleach, the evaluators spend time in a heroin "shooting gallery." Although they bring a tape recorder with them, they rarely use it. They find that although needles are being cleaned, a common dish is used to rinse needles and dilute the drug before shooting. A recommendation is made to alter the community's program to recognize the dangers of using the common dish.

Comment: The evaluators are observers of the shooting gallery. They do not conduct systematic surveys of the participants in the gallery.

2. To evaluate the effectiveness of an education-counseling program for adults with mental illness, the evaluation team lives for 3 months in five residential communities. After taping more than 250 counseling sessions, the evaluators conclude that the quality varies greatly both within and among the communities, helping to explain the overall program's inconsistent results.

Comment: The evaluators tape the sessions and then interpret the results. The interpretations come after the data are collected; no effort is made to postulate advance hypotheses.

3. To evaluate the impact of a school-based health program for homeless children, the evaluators teach a cohort of children to keep diaries over a 3-year period. The evaluation finds that children in the program are much more willing to attend to the dangers of smoking and other drug use than children in schools without the program. The diaries reveal that children in the program are especially pleased to participate. The evaluators conclude that the children's enjoyment may be related to the program's positive outcomes.

Comment: The use of diaries is a primary qualitative tool. It allows participants to say how they feel in their own words.

4. An evaluation of the impact on the county of a program to improve access to and use of job retraining services asks "opinion leaders" to give their views. These people are known in the county to have expertise in providing, financing, and evaluating job training programs. The interviewers encourage the leaders to bring up any issues that concern them. These people reveal that improvements probably result more from a stronger economy than from access to services. After the interviews are completed, the evaluators conclude that major barriers to access and use continue to exist even though statistical registries reveal a decline in unemployment for some workers.

Comment: The experts are invited to give their own views; little attempt is made to oblige the opinion leaders to adhere to certain topics.

Participatory Evaluation

A **participatory evaluation** invites representatives of groups that will be affected by the study's results to join the evaluation team for certain activities. These activities may include selecting evaluation questions, setting standards, choosing measures, and keeping the evaluator up-to-date on daily activities. Participatory evaluations can be very helpful in educating people who are not familiar with the evaluation process, enlisting their support in data collection, and adding meaning to statistical findings. Participatory evaluations are not without limitations, however. They require the evaluator to have skills in working with disparate groups of people, and they need time and patience.

Evaluation Research, Program Development, and Policy Formation

Program evaluation traditionally has been viewed as a method of systematically collecting and analyzing data about a specific program in order to improve or assess its overall performance.

During the past few decades, however, this insular perspective on the purposes of evaluation has evolved into a more global one.

Since the 1980s, program evaluation has assumed a prominent position as a key component of education and other kinds of social and psychological research. In part, this rise is due to improvements in its methods, but the field also has attracted practitioners with expertise in scientifically analyzing programs so that program developers, researchers, and policymakers have access to a continually growing quantity of empirically based evidence.

No longer do evaluators have to tiptoe behind program developers and funders, hoping for permission to collect data. Evaluation has proven its usefulness to the extent that most federal and state programs require evaluations of new programs, and some foundations hire staff specifically to oversee evaluation activities. In addition, evaluations are newsworthy. On a single day—April 23, 1992—page 1 of the *New York Times* featured two evaluations: an evaluation of a U.S. program linking welfare payments to job training and an evaluation of the impact on children's knowledge of current events of commercial in-school television.

Despite the maturation of evaluation methods and uses and the interest in evaluation findings, some evaluation practitioners continue to assert that their discipline is only rarely a form of research. These practitioners claim that, at certain stages of program development, research of any kind is neither practical nor desirable. The example usually given to defend this view is that of a newly organized program that needs time to grow and to train its staff, the goals and objectives of which are evolving. During the beginnings of any new program, the example continues, evaluators may be called in to help reformulate the goals and reassess the validity of the original standards; research is irrelevant. Further, the argument continues, evaluators sometimes are asked to conduct "summative" evaluations. These are historical reviews of programs that take place after the programs have been in operation for some period of time, and the reviews are performed so that already-developed and "evaluatable" programs can be summed up and compared. Evaluatable programs are those in full operation.

The argument that evaluation is rarely, if ever, research is flawed because it assumes that evaluators are really program developers at the mercy of a "real" world that is inimical to research. It is true that some trained evaluators have the skills to participate in program development, monitoring, and review and that practical concerns sometimes render research difficult to pursue. However, it is nonetheless more likely that graduates of disciplines directly concerned with institutional organization and management are better trained in program development than are evaluators. Evaluators are likely to be most helpful and influential in providing scientific data applicable beyond the needs of a single intervention.

Evaluation is useful to policymakers only if it is a scientific endeavor with generalizable results. Policymakers regulate access to, delivery of, and reimbursement for programs. They may be legislators, philanthropic foundation leaders, and leaders in the fields of education, psychology, and social welfare. They can have little use for data on the specific issues that pertain to the implementation of a single program, the hiring and training of its staff, and the perfection of its goals and standards.

Researchers, too, benefit little if evaluators focus their efforts on arbitrarily selected testimony and uncontrolled case studies of single programs. Current researchers want to learn more about programs in education, psychology, and social welfare and how to deliver and appraise them. The most constructive way of providing valid data on quality, effectiveness, efficiency, and methods is to use scientific procedures to investigate programs. The ability to do this is the bailiwick of the program evaluator.

SUMMARY AND TRANSITION TO NEXT CHAPTER ON QUESTIONS AND STANDARDS

Evaluation is a diligent investigation of a program's characteristics and merits. Its purpose is to provide information on a program's objectives, activities, outcomes, impact, and cost. To conduct an evaluation means posing questions and setting standards for a program's effectiveness, deciding on the design and sampling, and collecting, analyzing, interpreting, and reporting information. Evaluation information is used by financial supporters of programs, program developers, policymakers, and other evaluators and researchers. Collecting interim or formative evaluation data may be misleading and expensive; proceed with caution. Process evaluations are usually useful.

Before deciding on the types of data to collect for an evaluation and the design for collecting them, the evaluator must decide on the evaluation questions and the standards by which program effectiveness will be appraised. The next chapter discusses the sources and statement of evaluation questions and standards. The chapter also explains where standards of program effectiveness come from and describes the principles behind the use of expert panels, a commonly used method of coming to agreement on standards. Experts often are used to resolve the controversy surrounding issues in education, psychology, and social action, and they are particularly useful in setting standards when statistical methods alone are insufficient.

EXERCISES: PROGRAM EVALUATION: A PRELUDE

Directions

Read the example below and, using only the information offered, answer these questions:

1. What are the evaluation questions?
2. What are the standards?
3. What is the design?
4. What data collection measures are being used?
5. What additional information do you need to perform the evaluation?

Exercise: An Evaluation of
a Teacher Education Program (TEP)

Huntington-Ball University is concerned with improving its teacher education training program. Its first line of attack is high school teaching. An evaluation of the effectiveness of TEP is commissioned.

The evaluation team convenes a panel of teachers, administrators, curriculum planners, evaluators, and educational researchers to help identify the key competencies that should be evaluated. On the basis of the panel's suggestions and reviews of the current and proposed curriculum and published literature, the evaluation team decides on a plan of action. Each year, they will test and survey all participants in the proposed 2-year teacher training and internship program. The evaluation team also plans to observe trainees at least once a year from their entry into the program until 2 years after graduation.

Compared with previous graduates, participants in TEP are expected to be more versatile in their teaching methods and more knowledge-able in the subject they teach; most important, student performance should meet acceptable standards. The evaluators also plan to investigate whether the curriculum is equally successful for trainees of differing ages, interests, and experience.

A report will be available 6 months after the conclusion of the program.

Suggested Readings

Alkin, M., & Solomon, L. C. (1983). Conducting benefit-cost analysis of program evaluation. In M. Alkin & L. C. Solomon (Eds.), *The costs of evaluation.* Beverly Hills, CA: Sage.

An early but still relevant introduction to evaluating benefits and costs.

Fink, A. (1993). *Evaluation fundamentals: Guiding health programs, research, and policy.* Newbury Park, CA: Sage.

Explains the uses and methods of evaluation in health settings. Discusses qualitative and quantitative methods and the uses of evaluation in program development, research, and policy.

Herman, J. L., Morris, L. L., & Fitz-Gibbon, C. T. (1987). Evaluator's handbook. In J. L. Herman (Ed.), *Program evaluation kit* (2nd ed.). Newbury Park, CA: Sage.

A very good overview of evaluation purposes, methods, and uses.

Joint Committee on Standards for Educational Evaluation. (1994). *Program evaluation standards: How to assess evaluations of educational programs* (2nd ed.). Newbury Park, CA: Sage.

Distinguished evaluators and evaluation organizations have produced standards for evaluations that are technically sound and that serve the needs of their intended users in a cost-effective, ethical manner.

Kosecoff, J., & Fink, A. (1982). *Evaluation basics*. Newbury Park, CA: Sage.

Gives an overview of the methods and purposes of program evaluation.

Levin, H. M. (1983). *Cost-effectiveness: A primer*. Beverly Hills, CA: Sage.

Exactly what it says it is: a primer. Highly recommended for an introduction to the actual concepts of costs and effectiveness, and the relationship between the two.

Patton, M. Q. (1987). *How to use qualitative methods in evaluation*. Newbury Park, CA: Sage.

Tells when to use qualitative methods and how to design qualitative evaluations; discusses fieldwork and observation, in-depth interviewing, and how to analyze and interpret qualitative data.

Rossi, P. H., & Freeman, H. E. (1993). *Evaluation: A systematic approach*. Newbury Park, CA: Sage.

A basic text on the context and purposes of evaluation. An excellent discussion on cost-benefit and cost-effectiveness evaluation.

Scriven, M. (1967). The methodology of evaluation. In R. W. Tyler, R. M. Gagne, & M. Scriven (Eds.), *Perspectives of curriculum evaluation.* Chicago: Rand McNally.

This early essay by Michael Scriven is a classic, containing the first explanations of formative and summative evaluation. Practically anything by Michael Scriven is worth reading (although not always easy to read).

Scriven, M. (1993). *Hard-won lessons in program evaluation* (New Directions for Program Evaluation, No. 58). San Francisco: Jossey-Bass.

Useful discussion of the need to take into account an evaluation's political and social context.

Shadish, W. R., Cook, T. D., & Leviton, L. C. (1991). *Foundations of program evaluation: Theories of practice.* Newbury Park, CA: Sage.

Explains the theories and principles of program evaluation that have shaped the uniqueness of the field. If you want to learn (without going to the original sources) what the pioneers in the field have written, this is the book to read. It also contains a first-rate summary of evaluation as a special discipline rather than simply as applied social science.

Review Notes

Purpose of This Chapter

This chapter explains the characteristics of evaluation questions and how to set standards. It discusses the major purpose of evaluation questions, which is to provide data on the characteristics and merits of programs. Standards are the criteria for appraising effectiveness. They can be set statistically, but the evaluator must be careful to check them for practical meaning. The chapter also reviews the special role of experts in setting standards. Experts can provide insights into practical meaning when data alone are unavailable or insufficient. The relationships among evaluation questions and standards and the independent and dependent variables also are examined and summarized in a chart that visually depicts the connections.

2 Evaluation Questions and Standards

THE FIRST STEP

A Reader's Guide to Chapter 2

Evaluation Questions:
   Goals and objectives; participants and effectiveness;
   program activities, organization, and effectiveness;
   economics and costs; program environment

Setting Standards:
   Using experts, historical data, comparisons, and norms

Evaluation Questions and Standards

When to Set Standards

The QSV Reporting Form: Questions, Standards, and
Variables

Evaluation Questions

GOALS AND OBJECTIVES

Evaluation questions provide data on a program's characteristics and merits. In most evaluations, a main concern is to determine whether a program's goals and objectives have been met. The goals usually are meant to be relatively general and long term, as shown in Example 2.1:

Example 2.1. Typical Program Goals

For the Public

   Improve their quality of life

   Foster their improved intellectual, social, and psychological functioning

   Enhance their satisfaction with the schools and other social and mental health service providers

For the Professions

   Promote their research

   Enhance their knowledge

   Support their access to new technology and practices

   Improve their performance

   Improve their education

   Foster their efficiency

For Institutions

   Improve their organization, structure, and efficiency

   Optimize their ability to deliver accessible high-quality and superior education and mental health and other social services

For the System

Expand its capacity to provide high-quality education and mental health and other social programs

Support its efficiency

Ensure its respect for the educational, mental health, and social needs of all citizens

---

Objectives refers to the specific purposes that a program plans to achieve. Consider the excerpts from the description of a new course, given in Example 2.2.

Example 2.2. The Objectives of a New Course

The new two-semester course is designed to teach first- and second-year graduate students to conduct evaluations of education programs. Among the primary aims is to develop a handbook that teaches students the basic principles of evaluation and that offers an annotated bibliography so that more information can be obtained when needed. At the conclusion of the two semesters, students will be expected to plan the evaluation of a program. Each plan is to include evaluation questions, standards, study design and sampling methods, and data collection instruments.

Based on this excerpt, the objectives are:

For the curriculum developer:

♦ To produce an evaluation handbook with an annotated bibliography

For the student:

♦ To prepare an evaluation plan that includes questions, standards, research design, sampling methods, and data collection measures

Objectives can be aimed at any of the users or participants in the evaluation: teachers, students, institutions (e.g., schools, colleges, universities), funders, and the system itself. The users of evaluation results sometimes are called "stakeholders" because they have a "stake" or interest in the findings.

The evaluation questions for the program evaluation course might include the following two questions:

1. Was a program evaluation handbook produced?
2. Did students prepare an evaluation plan with questions, standards, study design, sampling, and data collection measures?

The identification of these two questions immediately raises additional questions: By when should the handbook be produced? How will we determine whether it is any good? What are the characteristics of a satisfactory evaluation plan, and who will judge it? How many students must prepare a satisfactory evaluation plan? These questions must be answered in subsequent evaluation activities. In the next step of the evaluation, for example, we consider ways of setting standards for determining achievement of objectives and program effectiveness and efficiency.

When identifying evaluation questions based on goals and objectives, the evaluator must be certain that all important goals and objectives have been identified, that the evaluation questions cover all important objectives, and that all questions can be answered with the resources available.

PARTICIPANTS AND EFFECTIVENESS

Evaluation questions often aim to describe the demographic and social characteristics of participants in a program and to link effective outcomes to specific participants. An evaluator might be asked, for example, to determine whether an arts program was effective with all children or only a portion—say, children under 12 years of age. Returning to the new program evaluation course, consider the questions about the program's participants given in Example 2.3.

Example 2.3. Evaluation Questions, Participants, and Program Effectiveness

The new evaluation course for first- and second-year graduate students was concerned with determining whether the program was effective for all types of students. One measure of effectiveness was the students' ability to prepare a satisfactory evaluation plan. The evaluator asked the following evaluation questions:

- What are the students' demographic characteristics?
- Is the program equally effective for differing students (e.g., males and females)?
- Do first- and second-year students differ in their learning?
- At the end of their second year, do the present first-year students maintain their learning?

Evaluation questions should be answerable with the resources available. Suppose the evaluation were only a 1-year study. Then the evaluator could not answer the question whether this year's first-year students maintained their learning during the next year. Practical considerations often temper the ambitions of an evaluation.

PROGRAM ACTIVITIES, ORGANIZATION, AND EFFECTIVENESS

Learning about a program's specific activities and its organization is frequently important in understanding a program's success or failure and whether it is applicable to other settings. Typical questions that focus on the program's activities and organization are:

- What were the key activities?
- To what extent were the activities implemented as planned?
- How well was the program administered?
- Did the program's influence carry over to other programs? institutions? consumers?
- Did social, political, or financial circumstances change so as to influence the effectiveness of the program?

Consider the case study given in Example 2.4, in which specific questions are posed about program activities and organization.

Example 2.4. Evaluation Questions, Activities, and Organization

A nine-member panel of experts in education, teaching, and evaluation met to define the kinds of learning that are appropriate for a course in program evaluation. The evaluation of the course is to take place during a 4-year period to enlist two groups of first- and second-year graduate students. Several of the best instructors were selected to help design the curriculum and the handbook and to teach the course. The evaluator asks:

- To what extent is the selection of the best teachers responsible for the quality of student learning and of the handbook?
- Does the new course affect students' subsequent education activities?
- During the 4-year period of the evaluation, do any changes occur in the school's support for the program or in the number and types of faculty who were willing to participate?

ECONOMICS AND COSTS

Program evaluations can be designed to answer questions about the resources that are consumed to produce program outcomes. The resources—costs—may be money, personnel, equipment, time, and facilities (e.g., offices, buildings). The outcomes may be monetary (e.g., the number of dollars saved) or substantive (e.g., better reading). When questions focus on the relationship between costs and monetary outcomes, the evaluation is termed a "cost-benefit analysis." When questions are asked about the relationship between costs and substantive outcomes, the evaluation is called a "cost-effectiveness evaluation."

Cost-Effectiveness: What are the comparative costs of Truancy Programs A and B in reducing daytime burglaries?

Cost-Benefit: For every $100 spent on the new truancy prevention program, how much is saved on reducing the costs of police protection for local businesses?

Questions about costs are asked relatively infrequently in evaluations for a number of reasons; among them are difficulties in defining costs and measuring benefits. Experts disagree about the best analytic methods to use to answer cost questions and whether an analysis should be conducted as part of the overall evaluation or as a separate study. When conducted concurrently, the economic analysis may add additional complexities to an already complex evaluation design; also, studying the costs of an intervention of (as yet) unproven effectiveness may not be warranted. Separate analyses, however, have the disadvantage of requiring a potentially different, second study. Example 2.5 illustrates the kinds of questions that program evaluators pose about costs, effects, benefits, and efficiency.

Example 2.5. Evaluation Questions: Costs

1. What is the relationship between the cost and effectiveness of three school staffing models? Costs include hourly salaries, benefits, rent, legal fees and insurance, supplies and equipment, and transportation. Outcomes (effectiveness) include teacher, student, and parent satisfaction and student achievement.

2. How efficient are the school health clinics? **Efficiency** is defined as the relationship between the use of practitioner time and the size of a clinic, waiting times for appointments, and time spent by practitioners in the clinic.

3. How do the most profitable private schools differ from the least profitable in terms of whether they are for-profit or nonprofit, number of scholarship students, enrollment numbers, endowments and donations, location, facilities, and number and qualifications of staff?

4. To what extent does each of three programs to retrain workers produce an annual savings in reduced unemployment claims that is greater than the annual cost of operating the program? The **benefits** are costs per worker (the costs of operating the program in each year, divided by the number of workers being trained that year). Because estimates of program costs are produced over a given 2-year period but estimates of savings are produced in a different (later) period, benefits have to be adjusted to a standard year. To do this, the total claims paid in each calendar year are adjusted by the consumer price index for unemployment compensation to a standard 1995 dollar. The costs of operating the programs are adjusted similarly to 1995 dollars by using the same index.

As can be seen from these questions, costs and effectiveness or benefits must be defined, and when appropriate, the value of the monetary costs must be described. Evaluators who answer questions about the costs of programs sometimes perform a "sensitivity analysis" when measures are not precise or the estimates are uncertain. Suppose that, in a study of the comparative cost-effectiveness of two state-funded school-based health care programs, the evaluators analyze the influence of increasing each program's funding first by 5% and then by 10%. In this case, the evaluators are testing the "sensitivity" of the program's effectiveness to changes in funding level. With this analysis, the evaluators will be able to tell whether increases in measures of effectiveness keep pace with increases in costs.

PROGRAM ENVIRONMENT

All programs take place in institutional, social, and political environments. Program A, which aims to improve the mathematical skills of children under age 14, for example, takes place in rural schools and is funded by the federal government and the state. Program B has the same aim; however, it takes place in a large city and is supported by the city and a private foundation.

If an evaluation takes place over several years (say, 3 or more), the social or political environment can change. New people and policies may emerge, and these may influence the program and the evaluation. Environmental changes that have affected programs in education include alterations in management practices, experiments with vouchers, and discoveries of new technologies.

When evaluating a program's environment, consider collecting data on the program's setting and funding as illustrated in Figure 2.1.

In addition to asking questions about a program's settings and funding, questions about program management and politics are relevant:

♦ *The managerial structure.* Who is responsible for the program's outcomes? How effective is the managerial structure? If the individuals or groups running the program were to leave, would the program continue to be effective?

♦ *The political context.* Is the political environment (meaning within or outside the institution) supportive of the success of the program? Is the program well funded?

Program/Intervention Settings

Geographic location(s):

A. Country: B. State(s):   C. Local (e.g., county/city)
  [ ] U.S.   1. ___ ___   1. _____
  [ ] European   2. ___ ___   2. _____
  [ ] Other, specify: 3. ___ ___   3. _____
  _____   4. ___ ___   4. _____
  _____   5. ___ ___   5. _____
                         (Enter up to five   [ ] CHECK HERE IF
                         different state   STUDY USED > 5
                         codes or   CITIES/COUNTIES
                         abbreviations)

                         [ ] CHECK HERE
                         IF STUDY USED
                         > 5 STATES

B. Funding Source(s): [ ] Federal government, specify:_____
(Check all that apply) [ ] State government, specify:_____
                       [ ] Local government (county/city), specify:___
                       [ ] Private foundation, specify:_____
                       [ ] Other, specify:_____
                       [ ] None stated

Figure 2.1. A Form to Survey the Program's Environment

Setting Standards

Program evaluations aim to provide convincing evidence that a program is effective. The **standards** are the specific criteria by which effectiveness is measured. Consider the following evaluation questions and their associated standards:

Evaluation question: Did students learn to formulate evaluation questions?

Standard: Ninety percent of all students in the new program will learn to formulate evaluation questions. Learning to formulate questions means identifying and justifying program goals and objectives and benefits and stating the question in a comprehensible manner. Evidence that the questions are comprehensible will come from review by at least three potential users of the evaluation.

AND

Evaluation question: Did the present group of first-year graduate students maintain their learning by the end of their second year?

Standard: No decreases in learning will be found between the second and first year.

In this case, unless 90% of the students learn to formulate questions by the end of the first year *and* first-year students maintain their learning over time, the evaluator cannot say the program is effective.

The standards are the key to the evaluation's credibility. The more specific they are, the easier they are to measure. To get at specificity, all potentially ambiguous terms in the evaluation questions and standards must be defined. Ambiguity arises when uniform definitions or levels of performance are unavailable. In the evaluation question "Has the School-to-Work Initiative improved students' preparation for the job market and decreased educational failure?" *improved preparation for the job market* and *decreased educational failure* are potentially ambiguous terms. To clarify the ambiguity, a dialogue like the one illustrated in Example 2.6 is helpful.

Example 2.6. Dialogue Between Evaluators in Clarifying Terms and Setting Standards

Evaluator 1 Improved means bettered or corrected.

Evaluator 2 For how many students and over what duration of time must improvement be shown?

Evaluator 1 Our experts are aiming for a statistically significant improvement in the attitudes, values, and knowledge needed to succeed in the workplace. We expect these gains to be sustained over a 5-year period. In addition, we aim for a statistically significant decrease in educational failure. For these students, educational failure means not acquiring the reading and math skills they need for entry-level jobs.

After clarifying terms, the evaluator might come up with standards like those given in Example 2.7 for the question "Has the School-to-Work Initiative improved students' preparation for the job market and decreased educational failure?"

Example 2.7. Illustrative Standards for Improved Preparation for the Job Market and Decreased Educational Failure

♦ When compared with students in two alternative programs, students in the initiative perform statistically significantly better in the following work-related skills: (They would be listed here.)

♦ No statistically significant differences are found over a 5-year period in participating students' ability to perform the following work-related activities: (They would be listed here.)

Structure, Process, and Outcome. A useful way to conceptualize standard-setting is to adapt the triumvirate that is used to evaluate the quality of health care: structure, process, and outcomes.

Structure refers to the organization and administrative environment in which programs take place and to the characteristics of personnel and supporting staff (e.g., including the number of teachers and their experience and educational and demographic backgrounds); setting (e.g., a public or private school, or classroom and workplace); and organization (e.g., how departments and teams are run).

Process means what is done to and for students and clients and includes the technical and humanistic or valuing aspects of education, counseling, service delivery, and so on. The processes encompass the methods and materials used to improve education and welfare.

Outcomes are the results or consequences of school and social systems, settings, and processes and include intellectual, social, psychological, and moral gains. Outcomes can be intermediate or conclusive. **Intermediate outcomes** are the direct results of the program; they can be seen and measured relatively quickly and easily. **Conclusive outcomes** take longer to occur and are more difficult to track and measure.

Example 2.8 gives illustrative standards for the evaluation question "Has the School-to-Work Initiative improved students' preparation for the job market and decreased educational failure?"

Example 2.8. Structure, Process, and Outcome Standards for an Evaluation Question About Preparation for the Job Market and for Decreasing Educational Failure

Structure Standards

- ◆ All teaching will be done by teams with three types of expertise: organizing work-study programs, teaching the subject matter (e.g., reading, math), and working with adolescents between 15 and 17 years of age.

- ◆ At least four local businesses will agree to provide work opportunities for at least 35% of the students in the program over a 2-year period.

Process Standards

- All students develop goals and objectives for their own course of study.
- Teachers, students, and employers will jointly develop methods for evaluating student progress.

Outcome Standards

Intermediate

- Significantly more students in the experimental program than in the control group will be able to read at grade level.
- At least 90% of the students will indicate that they are satisfied with the program.

Conclusive

- Five years after the program, 45% of the students in the program are employed full time.
- Five years after the program, at least 20% have received one or more promotions from their entry-level positions.

Standards must be purposeful; arbitrary standards may doom the program. Suppose the School-to-Work Initiative aimed to reduce the educational failure rate from 30% to 20%. If the rate decreased by only 5%, rather than 10%, would the program be a failure? What about 7%? The answer should by justified by data from other evaluations, the views and ideals of experts, and statistical comparisons.

In addition to being meaningful, standards of effectiveness should be realistic and measurable. Consider this evaluation question and standard.

Evaluation question: How do students in our school compare with students in other schools in their ability to write job applications?

Standard: A statistically significant difference in ability will be obtained, favoring our school.

Unless the evaluation has access to students in other schools and can test or observe them in the time allotted for the evaluation, this standard, though perhaps desirable, is unrealistic and cannot be used.

Standards for program evaluations can come from several sources: experts, historical data, comparisons with other groups and comparisons over time, and "norms."

USING EXPERTS

Experts can assist the evaluator in setting standards. **Experts are any individuals or representatives of professional, community, and other groups whose insights are likely to make the evaluation more useful or accurate.**

A variety of techniques are available for structuring group meetings to promote agreement among experts. These usually require the selection of a representative group of experts and the use of structured meetings. For example, if an evaluator is concerned with setting standards for a program to improve the quality of instruction in reading, then parents, students, curriculum developers, and experts in reading, education, psychometrics, and testing will be appropriate advisers.

Expert panels have been used extensively in other fields, such as health and medicine. For example, since 1977 the National Institutes of Health have used consensus development conferences to help resolve issues related to the knowledge and use of medical technology and the care of patients with such conditions as depression, sleep disorders, traveler's diarrhea, and breast cancer.

The main purpose of coming to "consensus" is to define levels of agreement on controversial subjects and unresolved issues. These methods are, therefore, germane to setting standards for judging the effectiveness of new programs for which no comparison group data are available. True consensus methods, however, are often difficult to implement because they typically require extensive reviews of the literature on the topic under discussion and highly structured methods.

Expert panels have proven to be effective in setting standards of performance, as illustrated in Example 2.9.

Example 2.9. Using Experts to Set Standards

Ten schools participated in a 4-year evaluation of a new middle school economics program. One of the program's objectives was to improve skills in organizing and presenting data in tabular form. A committee with members from the evaluation team, teachers, and the economics curriculum coordinators in each participating school district used data from other, similar programs and students to set standards of effectiveness. After 2 years, the evaluators presented interim data on performance and met with the committee to come to consensus on standards for the final 2 years of the study. To guide the process, the evaluators prepared the form shown in Figure 2.2.

Objective	Current Standard	Definitions	Interim Results	Question	Suggestion	Your Decision
Preparing accurate tables of data	When given raw data, 80% of students can put them accurately into tabular form.	An accurate table is divided into columns and rows. The most important comparisons are placed in the columns; statistical values are in ascending or descending order; key aspects of the tables are noted by using a convention (e.g., *, †, ‡).	50% of students can prepare an accurate table.	Is 80% reasonable?	On the basis of other students' performance, keep 80%.	____ %

Figure 2.2. Selected Portions of a Form Used in Setting Standards of Effectiveness

A number of methods relying on panels of experts have been used to promote understanding of issues, topics, and standards for program evaluation, but the most productive have depended on a few simple practices, as discussed in the following guidelines.

Guidelines for Expert Panels

1. The evaluation questions must be clearly specified. If they are not, the experts may help in clarification and in specification. Here are examples:

Not quite ready for standard-setting: Was the program effective with young children?

More amenable to standard-setting: Did the program improve the self-confidence of children between the ages of 3 and 5?

Standard: Significantly fewer children with poor self-confidence are found in the experimental versus the control group.

2. Data should be provided to assist the experts. These data can be about the participants in the experimental program, the intervention itself, and the costs and benefits of participation. The data can come from the published literature, from ongoing research, or from financial and statistical records. For example, in an evaluation of a program to improve school readiness among children from low-income families, experts might make use of information about the extent of the problem in the country. They also might want to know how prevalent lack of readiness is among children in low-income families, whether other interventions have been used effectively, and what their costs were.

3. The experts should qualify for selection because they are knowledgeable, are influential, or will use the findings. The number of experts to choose is necessarily dependent on the evaluation's resources and the evaluator's skill in coordinating groups. Example 2.10 gives two illustrations of the choice of experts.

Example 2.10. Choosing Experts to Set Evaluation Standards

♦ The Parent and Teacher Council aimed to improve relations among the major cultural groups whose children attended Lemberg Elementary School. An evaluation team was hired to direct and study the process and outcomes. The team asked each of the 10 council members to nominate three individuals to participate in an expert panel whose responsibility was to make recommendations. The evaluators selected 15 individuals whose names appeared on the lists at least twice.

♦ The primary goals of the Adolescent Outreach Program are to teach teens about preventive health and to ensure that all needed health care services (e.g., vision screening, immunizations) are provided. A group of teens participated in a teleconference to help the program developers and evaluators decide on the best ways to teach teens and to set standards of learning achievement. Also, physicians, nurses, teachers, and parents participated in a conference to determine the types of services that should be provided and the numbers of teens that should receive them.

---

4. The process should be carefully structured and skillfully led. A major purpose is to agree on the criteria for appraising a program's performance. To facilitate agreement and to distinguish the panel process from an open-ended committee meeting, an agenda should be prepared in advance, along with all materials (e.g., literature reviews, other presentations of data). It helps to focus the panel members on particular tasks, such as asking them to review a specific set of data and to rate the extent to which the set applies to the present program. For example, the experts can be given data on past performance (e.g., 75% of students could interpret the results of at least two of three tables) and be asked to rate the extent to which that standard should still apply (e.g., strongly agree, agree, disagree, strongly disagree).

USING HISTORICAL DATA OR PAST PERFORMANCE

The past performance of a group (or a similar group) sometimes is used as a standard against which to investigate a program's merits. However, this approach to standard-setting has some problems. History does not often repeat itself exactly. As a result, any standards based on previous performance, even with very similar programs and participants, may turn out to be inappropriate. Sometimes, the new standards will be too low; at other times, they may be too high.

USING COMPARISONS

Comparative standards are among the most convincing of standards. Comparisons can be made of one group's performance over time, among several groups' performance at one time, or among several groups' performance over time. It is sometimes difficult, however, to constitute similar comparison groups, engage their cooperation, and also have sufficient duration of time for observing differences, if any truly exist. It is extremely important to note that because an evaluation finds that one group is different from the other and that the difference favors the new program, one cannot automatically assume an effective program is at work. At least three questions must be asked before any such judgment is possible:

1. Were the groups comparable to begin with? (After all, by coincidence, one group might be smarter, more compliant, and so on.)

2. Is the magnitude of the difference large enough to be meaningful? With very large samples, small differences (e.g., in scores on a standardized test of achievement) can be statistically, but not educationally, significant.

3. Are the final levels of performance meaningful? For example, if you find significant changes in attitudes over time, you must consider also whether the extent of change is large enough to have educational and practical implication; even large changes may still be insufficient.

USING NORMS

Norms can serve as standards. If you know how other sixth graders in the nation read, for example, then you can use that reading level as a gauge for evaluating the effectiveness of a new statewide program that aims to raise it. Example 2.11 shows the use of norms as a standard in program evaluation.

Example 2.11. Using Norms as Standards in Program Evaluation

The new economics and business curriculum has been in existence in the Hart School District for 5 years. For the first 3 years, students showed little interest, and performance and attitudes were relatively low. For example, of all eligible students, only 35% were willing to take a class in economic forecasting. In nearby Mittman School District, the forecasting class is among the most popular, with about 78.5% of eligible students competing for very limited space. Mittman is similar to Hart in size and resources, so the 78.5% was considered a reasonable standard to apply in evaluating Hart's curriculum.

When using norms as a standard of comparison, one must make certain they are truly applicable. The only available data may have been collected at other times and under different circumstances and simply may not apply. For example, data gleaned from an evaluation conducted with young children may not apply to older children; if with older children, the findings may not apply to teens.

Evaluation Questions and Standards

An evaluation question may have one standard or several associated with it:

Question: Did students learn to review the literature reliably?

Standard 1: Eighty percent of all students learn to review the literature reliably.

Standard 2: A statistically significant difference in ability to review the literature is observed between students in School A and those in School B. Students in School A have participated in a new program, and the difference is in their favor.

The purpose of the two standards in this example is based on the view that if 80% of students in School A are found able to review the literature reliably, you cannot really attribute this positive result to a program unless you have access to the reviews of students who were not in a program. After all, nearly all students might know, from the start, how to review the literature. So why not rely solely on the second standard? Because differences alone, no matter how great, may not be enough.

Suppose students' learning in School A was actually significantly higher than in School B. If the level of both groups was low (say, average scores of 50% in the new program group and 20% in the comparison), then the difference, though statistically meaningful, might not be educationally meaningful and thus has little practical merit. You can conclude, for example, that even though the program successfully elevated performance, the amount of improvement was insufficient; the program was not worthwhile.

When to Set Standards

Standards should be in place before continuing with the evaluation's design and analysis. Consider this:

EXAMPLE 1

Program goal: To teach students to reliably review the literature

Evaluation question: Have students learned to reliably review the literature?

Standard: Ninety percent of all students learn to reliably review the literature.

Program effects on: Students

Effects measured by: Reliable reviews

Design: A survey of students' reviews

Data collection: A test of students' ability to review the literature

Statistical analysis: Compute the percentage of students who reliably review the literature.

EXAMPLE 2

Program goal: To teach students to reliably review the literature

Evaluation question: Have students learned to reliably review the literature?

Standard: A statistically significant difference in learning is observed between students in Schools A and B. Students in School A have participated in a new program, and the difference is in their favor.

Program effects on: Students in School A

Effects measured by: Reliable reviews

Design: A comparison of two groups of students

Data collection: A test of students' ability to review the literature

Statistical analysis: A *t* test to compare average review scores between Schools A and B

The evaluation questions and standards prescribe the evaluation's design, data collection, and analysis. They do this because they contain the independent and dependent variables on which the evaluation's design, measurement, and analysis are subsequently based.

Independent variables sometimes are called "explanatory" or "predictor variables." Because they are present before the start of the program or independent of it, evaluators use them to "explain" or "predict" outcomes. In the example above, reliable reviews of the literature (the outcome) are to be explained by students' participation in a new program (the independent variable). In evaluations, the independent variables often are the program (experimental and control), demographic features of the participants (e.g., gender, income, education, experience), and psychosocial and cultural characteristics (e.g., mental and social attributes, religious and cultural beliefs).

Dependent variables, also termed "outcome variables," are the factors the evaluator expects to measure. In educational program evaluations, these include knowledge, skills, attitudes, behavior, costs, and efficiency.

The evaluation questions and standards necessarily contain the independent and dependent variables: those on whom the program is to have an effect and measures of those effects, as illustrated in Example 2.12.

Example 2.12. Questions, Standards, and Independent and Dependent Variables

Program goal: To teach students to reliably review the literature

Evaluation question: Have students learned to reliably review the literature?

Standard: A statistically significant difference in learning is observed between students in Schools A and B. Students in School A have participated in a new program, and the difference is in their favor.

Program effects explained by (independent variable): Participation versus no participation in a new program

Effects measured by this outcome (dependent variable): Reliable review

---

The QSV Reporting Form:
Questions, Standards, and Variables

The relationship among questions, standards, and variables can be depicted in the evaluation questions, standards, and variables report. This report is useful for planning the evaluation and accounting for its methods. The report takes the form of a chart with four columns. The first states the evaluation questions; the second, the standards associated with each question; the third, the independent variables that structure the design; and the fourth, the dependent variables.

The QSV report is illustrated for a school-based, teacher-delivered curriculum to favorably modify health-related knowledge, beliefs, and self-confidence concerning health promotion and disease prevention among an eligible population of high school students from various racial and ethnic backgrounds in a large American city. Boys and girls in the 9th and 11th grades in two pairs of demographically similar high schools are assigned to receive either a special six-lesson health promotion program (experiment) or no formal curriculum (control).

The special curriculum—Health Assessment and Prevention Program for Youth (HAPPY)—focuses on conveying facts about healthful behaviors and risky ones and teaching skills necessary to practice good health habits. The main outcomes are measured by studying knowledge, beliefs, self-confidence, and behaviors (see Figure 2.3). The measures take place just before the start of the curriculum and within 3 months of its completion.

The QSV chart extracts the questions, standards, and variables from the description of the evaluation of HAPPY. The evaluation questions focus on the effectiveness of the program. Effectiveness is defined in two ways: finding a statistically significant difference (a) over time and (b) between the experimental and control groups. The independent or explanatory variable is group participation. The dependent or outcome variables are knowledge, beliefs, self-confidence, and behaviors. Example evaluation questions for HAPPY are:

Evaluation Questions	Standards	Independent or Explanatory Variables	Dependent or Outcome Variables
How effective is the program in favorably modifying knowledge, beliefs, self-confidence, and behaviors regarding health promotion and disease prevention?	A statistically and educationally significant improvement over a 6-month period for experimental students A statistically and educationally significant difference	Group participation (experimental and control students)	Knowledge, beliefs, self-confidence, behaviors

Figure 2.3. The Questions, Standards, and Variables (QSV) Reporting Form: Excerpts From an Evaluation of HAPPY, a High School Curriculum

How effectively does HAPPY favorably modify knowledge, beliefs, self-confidence, and behaviors for:

1. experimental and control students?
2. boys and girls?
3. 9th graders and 11th graders?

SUMMARY AND TRANSITION TO NEXT CHAPTER ON EVALUATION RESEARCH DESIGN

Evaluations are conducted to determine whether a program has merit. Was it worth the costs, or might a more efficient program accomplish even more? Evaluation questions focus the evaluation. They may be about the program's environment; the extent to which program goals and objectives have been met; the degree, duration, and distribution of benefits and effects; and the implementation and effectiveness of program activities and management strategies.

Program evaluations are concerned with providing convincing evidence that a program is effective. The standards are the specific criteria according to which effectiveness is established. Standards should be set in advance of any evaluation activities because they prescribe the evaluation's design, data collection, and analysis. One question may have more than one standard associated with it. Standards come from experts, the literature, past performance, normative data, and statistical comparisons.

The next chapter explains how to design an evaluation so that any changes in knowledge, attitudes, beliefs, and behaviors can be linked to an experimental program, and not to other competing events. For example, suppose you were evaluating a curriculum to improve students' knowledge of current events. You might conclude, erroneously, that your program was effective because students performed better on current events quizzes, unless the evaluation's design were sufficiently sophisticated to distinguish between the effects of the curriculum and other sources of education, such as television and newspapers. The next chapter discusses the most commonly used evaluation research designs.

EXERCISES: EVALUATION QUESTIONS AND STANDARDS: THE FIRST STEP

Directions

1. Read the example below and, using only the information offered, list the evaluation questions.

The district's Curriculum Department was concerned that its textbooks be up-to-date and accurate. Accordingly, the Committee on Textbook Accuracy (COTA) was formed and established guidelines for selecting textbooks for required and optional use from preschool through 12th grade. The district sponsored a series of in-service workshops in the use of the guidelines and the selection of texts. After 2 years, an evaluation was conducted. Among the hoped-for outcomes was that all teachers used the guidelines.

2. Read the example below and state the evaluation question and associated standards and the independent and dependent variables.

The Parent-Teacher Alliance is concerned that students in the district are required to participate in many untried experimental programs. As part of their participation, students are given numerous tests and surveys. The alliance is concerned that all personnel be made acutely aware of some of the ethical issues involved in experimentation, especially those pertaining to student privacy. The alliance is working with the district's newly formed Ethics Committee to formulate a program, institute it, and monitor its effects on staff each year for 5 years.

Suggested Readings

Cousins, J. B., & Earl, L. M. (1992). The case for participatory evaluation. *Educational Evaluation and Policy Analysis, 14,* 397-418.

An overview of the arguments for including stakeholders in key evaluation activities.

Donabedian, A. (1980). *Explorations in quality assessment and monitoring.* Ann Arbor, MI: Health Administration Press.
Donabedian, A. (1982). *The definition of quality and approaches to its assessment.* Ann Arbor, MI: Health Administration Press.
Donabedian, A. (1983). *The criteria and standards of monitoring.* Ann Arbor, MI: Health Administration Press.

These three volumes contain the classic definitions and explanations of how to assess quality of care in terms of its structure, process, and outcome.

Fink, A., Kosecoff, J., & Brook, R. H. (1986). Setting standards of performance for program evaluations: The case of the teaching hospital general medicine group practice program. *Evaluation and Program Planning, 9,* 143-151.

Describes the methods and usefulness of setting standards in a national study to improve the quality of care and education for health care practitioners.

Greene, J. G. (1988). Stakeholder participation and utilization in program evaluation. *Evaluation Review, 12,* 96-116.

Discusses the roles of stakeholders in program evaluation.

Joint Committee on Testing Practices. (1988). *Code of fair testing practices for education.* Washington, DC: American Psychological Association.

Sets standards for respecting the ethical responsibilities of testing in educational programs.

Review Notes

Purpose of This Chapter

An **evaluation design** is a structure created especially to produce an unbiased appraisal of a program's merits. The structure is built on the independent variables and the frequency and timing of measurement. This chapter discusses the relationships among evaluation designs and the evaluation questions and standards. It also explains the uses and limitations of experimental and observational evaluation designs. The role of the evaluation design chart in establishing the logical connections between the purposes and methods of the evaluation also is discussed.

3 Designing Program Evaluations

Evaluation Design: Creating the Structure

An **evaluation design** is a structure created especially to appraise a program's effectiveness objectively and without bias. Consider Examples 3.1, 3.2, and 3.3.

Example 3.1. Evaluation Design: The Same Group Is Measured Over Time

Narrative: A new Spanish-language writing program for fifth graders is being evaluated in the district's 12 elementary schools. If effective, it will replace the traditional program. A key evaluation question is whether participating students' knowledge improves. To be eligible for participation, students must read at the fifth-grade level or better in Spanish. Improvement is to be analyzed statistically. Students will be tested within 1 month of the beginning of the program and again after 1 year to determine how much is learned.

Abstract

   Program: A new fifth-grade Spanish-language writing program

   Evaluation question: Does students' knowledge improve?

   Standard: Statistically significant improvement over time

   Independent variable: Students in the new program

   Eligibility for evaluation: All 12 elementary schools are eligible.

   Eligibility for the program: Students must read at the fifth grade or better in Spanish.

   Measurement: A test of students' knowledge within 1 month of the beginning of the experimental program; a test of the same students' knowledge 1 year after completion of the program

---

Example 3.2. Evaluation Design With Random Selection and Measurement Over Time

Narrative: A new Spanish-language writing program for fifth graders is being evaluated in 6 of the district's 12 elementary schools, to be selected at random. If effective, the program will be introduced throughout the district's 12 elementary schools. A key evaluation question is whether students' knowledge improves. To participate, students must read at the fifth-grade level or better in Spanish. Improvement is to be analyzed statistically. Students will be tested within 1 month of beginning the program and after 1 year to determine how much is learned.

Abstract

Program: A new fifth-grade Spanish-language writing program

Evaluation question: Does students' knowledge improve?

Independent variable: Students in six elementary schools participating in a new program

Standard: Statistically significant improvement over time

Eligibility for the evaluation: 6 of 12 elementary schools in the district

Selection for the evaluation: Six schools will be selected at random.

Eligibility for the program: Students who read at the fifth-grade level or better in Spanish

Measurement: A test of students' knowledge within 1 month of the beginning of the experimental program; a test of the same students' knowledge 1 year after completion of the program

Example 3.3. Evaluation Design With Random Selection and Randomly Assigned Groups Measured Over Time

Narrative: A new Spanish-language writing program for fifth graders is being evaluated in six elementary schools. If effective, it will be introduced throughout the district's 12 elementary schools. The six participating schools will be chosen at random. Of the six, three will be assigned randomly to continue with their regular writing program, and students in the other three will participate in the new one. A key evaluation question is whether students' knowledge improves. Improvement is to be analyzed statistically. To participate, students must read at the fifth-grade level or better in Spanish. Students will be tested within 1 month of beginning the program and after 1 year to determine how much is learned.

Abstract

   Program: A new fifth-grade Spanish-language writing program

   Evaluation question: Does students' knowledge improve?

   Independent variable: Students in an experimental and in a control program

   Standard: Statistically significant improvement over time

   Eligibility for the evaluation: 6 of 12 elementary schools in the district

   Selection for the evaluation: Six schools will be selected at random.

   Eligibility for the program: Students who read at the fifth-grade level or better in Spanish

   Assignment to groups: Three schools will be assigned at random to the experimental program; the students in the other three schools will be assigned to continue with the traditional district-approved writing program.

   Measurement: A test of students' knowledge within 1 month of the beginning of the experimental program; a test of the same students' knowledge 1 year after completion of the program

In Example 3.1, all schools and eligible students will participate in the evaluation; they will be measured before and after
participation. In Example 3.2, six schools will be selected at random
to participate in the evaluation, and eligible students will be tested
before and after participation. In Example 3.3, three of the six
selected schools will be assigned at random into the new or experimental program; eligible students in the other three schools will
receive the regular program. Students in the third example also will
be measured twice: before and after the intervention.

These three examples are illustrative of three basic program
evaluation designs: (a) experimental evaluation designs with non-
random selection into the evaluation and relying on one group to act
as a control or comparison for itself (using a premeasure and a
postmeasure); (b) experimental evaluation designs with random
selection into the evaluation and relying on one group to act as a
control or comparison for itself (using a premeasure and a postmeasure); and (c) experimental evaluation designs with random selection into the evaluation and random assignment into experimental
and control groups and a premeasure and postmeasure.

Before designing an evaluation, at least six questions should be
answered. The questions are given below and are followed with
answers from the examples taken from the new Spanish-language
writing program.

Questions to Ask When Designing Evaluations

1. What are the evaluation question and its associated standards?
2. What are the independent variables?
3. What are the inclusion and exclusion criteria?
4. Will a control group be included?
4a. If yes, what are the characteristics of the control group?
5. When will measures be taken?
6. How often will measures be taken?

Selecting an Evaluation Design:
Dealing With the Six Questions

1. WHAT ARE THE EVALUATION QUESTION AND ITS ASSOCIATED STANDARDS?

A first step in the selection of any evaluation design is to turn to the evaluation question and its associated standards. The standards are the guide to a *minimum* design. If the standards call for changes over time, for example, you know that a design is needed in which two measurements are taken. This is the case for all three evaluation examples given above. In Example 3.3, however, the evaluation also combines the two measurements with two groups. The addition of a comparison group to a design always strengthens it. Suppose, for example, an evaluation found that fifth graders improved their writing ability after their participation in an experimental program. Unless the evaluator also can demonstrate that fifth graders in comparable programs do *not* improve, claims that the new program is effective can be challenged. Fifth graders can improve in their writing ability for several reasons, among them ordinary intellectual maturation.

2. WHAT ARE THE INDEPENDENT VARIABLES?

Independent variables are also called "explanatory" or "predictor variables" because they are used to explain or predict the program's outcomes (the dependent variables). They are independent of the program and are part of the evaluation's structure or design.

In evaluations, the independent variables are often group participation (experimental group and control groups) and the participants' socioeconomic status and educational status. The evaluator uses these variables in hypothesizing or predicting the outcomes (dependent variables) of program participation. Consider the relationship among the following evaluation questions, standards, independent variables, and outcomes.

Relationship Among Evaluation Questions, Standards, Independent Variables, and Outcomes

A. *Evaluation question:* How do participants in the experimental and control groups compare in their social activity?

> *Standard:* A statistically significant difference in social activity, favoring the experimental group
>
> *Independent variable:* Group participation (in the experimental or in the control group)
>
> *Outcome (dependent variable):* Social activity
>
> *Evaluator's prediction:* Participation in the experimental program will be associated with increased and higher quality social activity than participation in the control program.

B. *Evaluation question:* How do low-income children in the new Advance Start Program compare with low-income children in the traditional program in their readiness to read and write?

> *Standard:* A statistically significant difference between the new and traditional program, favoring the new program
>
> *Independent variable:* Group participation (in the new or traditional program)
>
> *Outcome (dependent variable):* Readiness for reading and writing
>
> *Evaluator's prediction:* Participation in the new program will be associated with increased readiness in reading and writing.

Once the evaluator has the questions, standards, independent variables, and outcomes, the design comes next.

Evaluation Question, Standards, Independent Variables, Outcomes, and Design

> *Evaluation question:* To what extent has the quality of the children's life improved after participation in the program?
>
> *Standard:* A statistically and practically significant improvement in quality of life between participating and nonparticipating boys and girls whose problems vary in complexity

Independent variables: Group participation, gender, age, and problems
Outcome (dependent variable): Quality of life
Design:

	Experimental	*Control*
Boys		
Very complex problems		
Average complexity		
Not very complex problems		
Girls		
Very complex problems		
Average complexity		
Not very complex problems		

The independent variables frame the design. In some cases, the frame is relatively easy to create because the categories are self-evident, as they are for gender (male and female) and group participation (experimental and control). But for other independent variables, such as age, complexity of problems, and parents' socioeconomic status, deciding on categories becomes more complicated. In this example, complexity of problems was divided into three categories: very complex, average, and not very complex. But other categories might have been chosen—for example, one to two, three to four, more than four. The choice of categories depends on what the literature says (Are data available that suggest the most accurate way to define problem complexity?) and resources (How many groups can you afford to include in the evaluation?).

3. WHAT ARE THE INCLUSION AND EXCLUSION CRITERIA?

Inclusion criteria (sometimes called "eligibility criteria") separate those who are eligible for participation in the evaluation from those who are not and are the foundation for inferring conclusions about the groups most likely to benefit from participation. For example, suppose an evaluation is commissioned to determine the effectiveness of a program to provide students with after-school computer practice. Students are eligible if they are between the ages of 10 and 12. Suppose also that the program cannot afford to provide transportation to the program's location. If the program is effective, the nature of the eligibility criteria necessarily will limit its applicability to students between the ages of 10 and 12 who have the means and motivation to arrange transportation. These children may be quite different from others in the incentives needed to get them to practice using computers after school.

Criteria for inclusion into an evaluation sometimes come from primarily practical considerations. These consist of such parameters as geographic and temporal proximity and demographic and health characteristics. Consider the illustrative inclusion criteria in Example 3.4.

Example 3.4. Illustrative Inclusion or Eligibility Criteria

Inclusion Criteria

For a writing program

- Schools with at least five teachers willing to participate
- Children who have written at least one poem

For a school-based family planning program

- School health clinics serving 50 or more students each week
- School health clinics serving 50 or more girls each week

Evaluations sometimes have **exclusion criteria**. These are special criteria that apply to potential participants whose inclusion is likely to impair the actual functioning of the evaluation or skew its data. Consider the sample exclusion criteria in Example 3.5.

Example 3.5. Illustrative Exclusion Criteria

Exclusion Criteria

For a writing program

♦ Schools whose fifth-grade writing program meets less often than once a week

For an after-school counseling program

♦ Children with serious disorders, such as autism and schizophrenia, who are unlikely to comply with program rules

---

In addition to practical considerations, eligibility criteria come from the evaluation questions, as illustrated in Example 3.6.

Example 3.6. Inclusion and Exclusion Criteria: The Evaluation Questions

Evaluation question: Has access to mental health services for high-risk families improved?

Ask: Which high-risk groups must be included for this program to receive a fair trial? To which high-risk groups are the findings to be applied? Where and when can I obtain these families for participation?

Example inclusion criteria:

Must live within 10 miles of the center

Teenage mothers with at least one other child living at home

Families with a record of child endangerment

Homeless families living in county-run shelters

Example exclusion criteria:

Families with private insurance that covers mental health

Families with incomes 250% above the federal poverty level

Evaluation question: Have students improved their writing ability?

Ask: What are the characteristics of students who must be included for this program to receive a fair trial? To which groups of students should the findings be applicable? Where and when can I get these students to participate?

Example inclusion criteria:

Must be in one of the district's elementary schools

Students whose reading abilities in Spanish are at the fifth-grade level or better

Example exclusion criteria:

Students whose teachers have less than 1 year experience teaching writing

Students with less than a grade point average of 3.0

Students who were absent in the past year an average of 5 or more days each month

---

4. WILL A CONTROL GROUP BE INCLUDED?

The term **group** refers to the institutions and individuals who participate in the evaluation, regardless of whether or not they

Experimental Group	Control Group

Figure 3.1. A Basic Evaluation Design: The Experimental and Control Groups Compared

receive the experimental intervention. A typical evaluation design consists of an experimental and a control group. The experimental group is given the new program; the control receives some other program. This is a fundamental design, and it can be represented as shown in Figure 3.1.

Some evaluations have more than one experimental group and more than one control group. For example, suppose an evaluation for a hypothetical new writing program for fifth graders wants to compare two styles of instruction: computer-assisted (Program A) and small group discussion (Program B). Suppose also that the evaluator proposes two control groups: teacher-directed lecture and discussion (Control 1) and self-instructional learning modules (Control 2). The design for this evaluation is depicted in Figure 3.2.

In an evaluation, what program should the control group receive? This very important question often is not given the attention it deserves. Frequently, the control program consists of the usual services or no services at all. A control group must start out to be demonstrably like the experimental group in its composition (behavior, knowledge, attitudes, demographic characteristics) but definably and measurably different in its program. Programs can differ in their philosophies, objectives, methods, settings, duration, management, and resources.

5. WHEN WILL MEASURES BE TAKEN?

In evaluations, measures can be made before and after the program, during the program, or just after. Premeasures can serve many important evaluation purposes, such as to select groups to participate in the evaluation and program, to check the need for the

	Experimental Program A: Computer-Assisted Instruction	Experimental Program B: Small Group Discussion
Control Program 1: Teacher directed		
Control Program 2: Self-instructional modules		

Figure 3.2. An Evaluation Design for a Program Comparing Instructional Methods: Two Experimental and Two Control Groups

NOTE: This design suggests 10 possible comparisons:
1. Program A with Program B
2. Program A with Program 1
3. Program A with Program 2
4. Programs A and B (the experiment) with Programs 1 and 2 (the control)
5. Program B with Program 1
6. Program B with Program 2
7. Programs A and B (the experiment) with Program 1
8. Programs A and B (the experiment) with Program 2
9. Programs 1 and 2 (the control) with Program A
10. Programs 1 and 2 (the control) with Program B

program, to ensure comparability of groups, and to provide a basis for calculating change or improvement. The merit of using premeasures can be compromised, however, if they are not demonstrably similar to the postmeasures, if they are administered very closely in time to the postmeasure (because people simply may repeat their responses from the premeasure), and if they influence program participants to behave or perform in special ways (by focusing people's attention on program content). Figure 3.3 gives illustrative uses of premeasures and postmeasures.

6. HOW OFTEN WILL MEASURES BE TAKEN?

The frequency of measurement should depend on how much time is needed for the program's effects to occur, the duration of the

Measure	Uses	Comments
Premeasure to select groups.	Students were tested for their ability to read Spanish in order to identify those with reading levels at fifth grade or better. A financial analysis was conducted to identify women eligible for welfare assistance.	Data like these (reading level and financial status) are often available from records. Using existing data can save time.
Premeasure to check the need for the program.	A pretest of students' knowledge revealed that they already knew a substantial portion of the information to be imparted in the new curriculum. A financial analysis revealed that more families are eligible than the original estimates for the new program suggested.	This information can be used to revise the program or the evaluation questions and standards.
Premeasure to ensure comparability of groups.	Schools A, B, and C, which volunteered for the program, were found to have more experienced writing teachers than Control Schools X, Y, and Z. No differences were found in the ages, marital status, education, or income of the volunteer experimental and control groups.	Differences between or among groups before the start of the program can easily bias the results. Determing the nature and extent of potential "contaminants" is essential in program evaluation.

continued

Figure 3.3. Illustrative Uses of Premeasures and Postmeasures

Measure	Uses	Comments
Premeasure to provide a basis for measuring change or improvement.	Students in the experimental group gained significantly more knowledge than those in the control group. Parents whose children were in the experimental group did not have higher incomes than parents whose children were in the control group.	Premeasures provide a baseline against which to measure progress for single groups ("self-controls") and for multiple groups.
Postmeasure to appraise benefit, outcome, impact, and cost.	Average scores on a test were compared between the experimental and control groups after participation in a writing program. Parents willing to participate were compared after half joined a parenting program.	Postmeasures provide evidence of a program's merits. They include achievement tests, surveys (interviews, telephone, self-administered questionnaires), observations, and record reviews.

Figure 3.3. (Continued)

program and the evaluation, and the resources available for measurement. The time needed to observe and measure a program's hoped-for effects varies according to the characteristics of the expected outcomes, impact, and costs. For example, assessing students at the end of a year to determine the effects of a program to teach specific writing content to fifth graders is probably reasonable. However, assessing changes in teens' health habits and associated costs at the end of 1 year would be foolhardy because these variables usually take longer than 1 year to observe. To identify the expected amount of time to uncover changes in health habits, practices, and costs, a literature review or survey of experts often is indicated.

Remember, the longer the period needed for measurement and observation, the more opportunity external effects (e.g., changes in how schools are organized and reimbursed, changes due to children's physical and social maturation) will have to interact with and "confound" the results.

Yearly measurement to search for long-term changes may be indicated, but programs and their evaluations rarely last more than 3 to 5 years. To ensure the possibility of continuous evaluation, a data collection system can be created and continuously updated.

Designs for Program Evaluation

Evaluations aim to be prospective investigations of a program's characteristics and effectiveness. In a prospective investigation, data are collected for the specific purposes of the evaluation, commencing with the start of the evaluation. To demonstrate this point, consider the illustrations in Example 3.7.

The best program evaluations are prospective because they are amenable to the most "control." Retrospective studies sometimes are called "summative evaluations." These are historical analyses and leave too much to chance to satisfy the demands of a diligent investigation of a program's characteristics and merits.

In Retrospective Study B (see Example 3.7), for example, assume that all high scorers were found to have participated in the district's new program. Can the evaluator conclude that the program was effective? Perhaps the high scorers were more knowledgeable to begin with. In Prospective Evaluation C, the positive findings can be a reflection of the characteristics of the initiative's participants, rather than a reflection of the effectiveness of the project (they may have been more motivated to begin with). Advance control over the contents of the program, over selection and assignment to groups, and over data collection is essential in ensuring the validity of an evaluation's findings.

Example 3.7. Evaluations Are Prospective

Prospective Evaluation A. An evaluation asked whether fifth-graders' knowledge improved after their participation in a writing program. A test was given to the students 1 month before the program started and 1 year after their participation. Performance was compared over time.

Retrospective Study B. For the past 5 years, the school district has administered an achievement test to all fifth graders to determine their knowledge of preventive health care. At the end of the fifth year, test records were reviewed to identify high and low scorers. The two groups were compared to determine whether a relationship existed between participation in a new program and scores.

Prospective Evaluation C. Does participation in the School-to-Work Initiative improve attitudes toward work? Data were collected on participants at the time of their entry into the initiative and 6 months after graduation. An evaluation was conducted that compared attitudes between participants and nonparticipants.

Retrospective Study D. Does participation in the School-to-Work Initiative improve attitudes toward work? The evaluation waited 3 years to compare the attitudes of participants and nonparticipants. No differences were found.

The following designs have been selected because they are most appropriate for program evaluations. Observational designs are included because they are used frequently in evaluations and have a major role to play in them. Because program evaluations borrow from a number of disciplines, you will find that several terms (e.g., **true experiment, randomized controlled, control trial**) sometimes are used synonymously by evaluators. These terms are explained as they are mentioned in the text.

A Classification of Program Evaluation Designs

I. *Experiments*

    A. *Concurrent controls in which participants are randomly assigned to groups.* These are called "randomized controlled" or "control trials" or "true experiments."

    B. *Concurrent controls in which participants are not randomly assigned to groups.* These are called "nonrandomized controlled trials" or "quasi experiments."

    C. *Self-controls.* These require premeasures and postmeasures and are called "longitudinal" or "before-and-after designs."

    D. *Historical controls.* These make use of data collected on participants in other surveys.

II. *Observational or Descriptive Designs*

    A. *Cross sections.* These provide descriptive data at one point in time.

    B. *Trends.* These provide data on a general population (e.g., American voters, high school students) at different points in time.

    C. *Cohorts.* These provide data on the same specific population (e.g., the graduating class of 1995, men who fought in the U.S. Army in the Vietnam War).

    D. *Case controls or matched controls.* These retrospective studies go back in time to help explain a current phenomenon.

EXPERIMENTAL EVALUATIONS

Evaluations With Concurrent Controls and Random Assignment: The True Experiment

With this evaluation design, a group of potential program participants (e.g., children over the age of 7, children in need of polio vaccinations, high-risk families) are identified. They then are assigned at random to the new program or the control. The program is introduced concurrently to both groups, and the two groups are compared on some outcome of interest (e.g., knowledge). This design sometimes is called a "randomized trial" or a "randomized controlled trial" or "control trial" or a "true experiment."

In some true experiments, the participants and evaluators sometimes do not know which group is the experimental one and which is the control: This is the **double-blind experiment**. When participants do not know but evaluators do, this is the **blinded trial**.

In evaluation studies, it is often logistically or ethically difficult to "blind" participants, introducing bias or error. Another potential source of bias is failure to deliver a uniform program. For example, if two professors are to teach the same content, their teaching styles may be so different as to "bias" the results.

The true experiment is the fundamental design against which others are judged because causation can be inferred from it. To ensure the generalizability of the results, true experiments of the same intervention probably should be conducted in many places, with a variety of participants, over a number of years.

From the evaluator's perspective, the experimental evaluation with randomly constituted concurrent controls is the ideal, but many factors mitigate against the use of this design:

♦ Evaluators typically lack the resources to conduct a multisite program.

♦ Evaluators have difficulty in getting enough participants to constitute groups.

♦ Evaluators are not granted the time and money needed to prepare and implement the design.

♦ A potential disparity invariably exists between the urgency with which data are needed and the amount of time required to conduct the evaluation.

♦ Ethical and other problems arise in randomly assigning and blinding participants and evaluators.

♦ In very large evaluations, it can be a logistical nightmare to ensure that the program and assessment measures (e.g., tests, surveys) are being implemented across groups in a uniform way.

Evaluations With Concurrent Controls
but No Randomization: The Quasi Experiment

Nonrandomized, concurrent controls (quasi-experimental designs) mean the creation of an experimental and a control group without random assignment. This design is usually easier to implement than a true experiment. Suppose you were the evaluator of a teacher training program. Each year, three teachers in six colleges will participate. The aim of the 3-year program is to enhance teachers' ability to teach English and American literature in schools with diverse cultural traditions. By the end of the third year, 54 teachers will have participated. In this example, because the numbers of teachers and colleges are relatively small, random assignment really does not make sense.

The use of nonrandomly selected controls in evaluation contains the possibility of bias from additional sources, as illustrated in Example 3.8.

Example 3.8. Biases of Concurrent Controls Without Randomization

Membership bias. This bias exists in preexisting groups (e.g., students at this college and students at another) because one or more of the same characteristics that cause people to belong to the groups (e.g., choice of colleges) are associated with the outcome being evaluated (e.g., attitude toward and knowledge of a particular subject matter).

Nonresponse bias. This bias occurs when participants are invited to volunteer to participate in an evaluation study. For example, suppose faculty are invited to participate in a new teacher education program. Those who accept may be somewhat different from nonaccepters in their willingness to try new educational programs, or they may have more time at the present to participate in a new activity, and so on.

Evaluations With Self-Controls:
Pre- and Posttests on One Group

A design with self-controls uses a group of participants to serve as its own comparison. Suppose, for example, an educational evaluator tested teacher trainees three times: (a) at the beginning of the year to find out how much they knew to begin with, (b) immediately after their participation in a new course to find out how much they learned, and (c) at the end of 2 years to ascertain how much learning they retained. This three-measurement strategy describes an evaluation design using the trainees as their own control. In the example, the evaluator measures the trainees once before and twice after the intervention (a new course). Designs of this type also are called "before-and-after" or "pretest-posttest designs."

Evaluations that use self-controls alone are prone to many biases. Without a control group, you cannot conclude that any observed effects are due to the program, rather than to inherent group qualities.

Among the biases associated with self-control designs is the **Hawthorne effect,** or the tendency to perform differently (and better) because of enthusiasm for a new program. Other possible influences include the physical, emotional, and intellectual maturity of the participants and historical or external events. For example, suppose teacher trainees in a new course are found to acquire important skills and to retain them over time. This finding may be due to the new course or to the characteristics of the trainees, who from the start may have been motivated to learn and excited by being in an experimental program. Also suppose that, during the year, a visiting professor gives several inspiring lectures to the teacher trainees. The trainees' performance on subsequent tests may be due as much or more to the lectures as to the program.

The soundness of self-controlled designs is also dependent on the appropriateness of the number and timing of measurements. To check on changes in attitude in a schoolwide program, for example, should students be surveyed once? twice? at what intervals? Interventions and programs can be judged to be ineffective solely because data were presented too soon for the hoped-for outcomes to occur.

Evaluations With Historical Controls:
Using Norms

Evaluations with historical controls rely on data that are available from some other, recorded source. Historical controls include established norms of height, weight, blood pressure, and scores on standardized tests, such as reading tests and the SATs. They also may consist of data from participants in other programs or the same program in another setting. Historical controls are convenient; their main source of bias is the potential lack of comparability between the group on whom the data were originally collected and the group of concern in the evaluation.

OBSERVATIONAL OR DESCRIPTIVE EVALUATIONS

Survey Designs

Evaluators use survey designs to collect baseline information on experimental and control groups, to guide program development, and as a source of data regarding the program and its environment. Survey designs enable the evaluator to present a cross-sectional portrait of one or many groups at one period of time. Example 3.9 illustrates survey designs in program evaluations.

Example 3.9. Survey Designs and Program Evaluation

1. *A test of student knowledge of program evaluation principles.* The Curriculum Committee wanted information on entering graduate students' knowledge of the methods and uses of program evaluation in improving education. They asked the evaluator to prepare and administer a brief test to all students. The results revealed that 80% of entering graduate students could not distinguish observational and experimental evaluation designs and that only 20% could list more than one source for setting standards of program effectiveness. The Curriculum Committee used the findings to

develop a course of instruction to provide entering graduate students with skills to conduct and review evaluations.

2. *A review of the attendees at workshops to train teachers and counselors to teach students about AIDS.* A review was conducted of the records of the attendees at 10 workshops offered to teachers and counselors in the school district. Attendance was voluntary and low. The data are being used to target a districtwide publicity campaign to get the highest possible number of attendees in future workshops.

3. *A survey of satisfaction with the teacher training program.* A survey was conducted of all graduates who were trained during the past 10 years at the Teacher Education Center. The findings revealed that nearly 70% of 500 respondents were females between 24 and 53 years of age. Just over 87% indicated they were very satisfied with their training; however, over 50% stated they would have liked more hands-on, practical experience. The findings suggest that the college needs to redirect its efforts to determine ways to provide future trainees with practical learning experiences.

Cohort Evaluations

A **cohort** is a group of people who have something in common and who remain part of a group over an extended period of time. Cohort studies ask "What will happen?" They are prospective designs, and the group is followed over time, or longitudinally.

In evaluations, the cohort consists of participants in a program who are observed over time to determine the extent to which the program's effects have lasted and how and to what extent program participation influenced the future. For example, a cohort of students in an experimental program to encourage them to teach can be monitored over time to determine how many become teachers and the extent to which they were motivated by their participation in the experiment.

Group 1	Premeasure	Program	Postmeasure
Group 2	Premeasure		Postmeasure
Group 3		Program	Postmeasure
Group 4			Postmeasure

Figure 3.4. The Solomon Four-Group Design

Cohort studies are expensive to conduct because they are long term and because they are subject to biases from selection (those who are chosen and willing to participate in the evaluation may be very different from those who do not participate) and attrition.

COMBINATIONS:
THE SOLOMON FOUR-GROUP DESIGN

Evaluation designs can involve two groups that are observed before and after an intervention. A very powerful evaluation design is the Solomon four-group, in which participants are assigned randomly to four groups. The design can be depicted as in Figure 3.4.

In this example, Groups 1 and 3 participated in a new program, but Groups 2 and 4 did not. Suppose the new program aimed to improve students' knowledge of U.S. constitutional history. Using the four-group design (and assuming an effective program), the evaluator can expect to find the following results:

1. In Group 1, knowledge on the postmeasure should be greater than on the premeasure.
2. More knowledge gain should be observed in Group 1 than in Group 2.
3. Group 3's postmeasure should indicate more knowledge than Group 2's premeasure.
4. Group 3's postmeasure should indicate more knowledge than Group 4's postmeasure.

This design is a true experiment (with randomly assigned groups), and it incorporates self- and concurrent controls.

Figure 3.5 is a review of seven major evaluation designs.

Evaluation Design	Benefits	Concerns
Concurrent controls and random assignment (randomized controlled or control trial; true experiment)	If properly conducted, can establish the extent to which a program caused its outcomes	Difficult to implement logistically and methodologically
Concurrent controls without randomization (quasi experimental)	Easier to implement than a randomized control trial/true experiment.	A wide range of potential biases may occur because, without an equal chance of selection, participants in the program may be systematically different from those in the controls. Also, the two groups in the evaluation may be systematically different from other, nonparticipating groups.
Self-controls or pre- and posttest	Relatively easy to implement logistically. Provide data on change.	Must be certain that measurements are appropriately timed. Without a control group, the evaluator cannot tell whether seemingly experimental effects are also present in the control group.
Historical controls or norms	Easy to implement; unobtrusive	Must ensure that "normative" comparison data are applicable to participants in the evaluation

continued

Figure 3.5. Review of Evaluation Designs: Benefits and Concerns

Evaluation Design	Benefits	Concerns
Survey designs (cross-sectional)	Provides baseline information on the evaluation's participants and descriptive information on the program and its setting and resources	Offers a static picture of participants and program at one point in time
Cohort	Provides longitudinal or follow-up information	Can be expensive because they are relatively long-term studies. Participants who are available over time may differ in important ways from those who are not.
Solomon four-group	Rigorous design that can enable evaluator to infer causation. Guards against the effects of the premeasure on subsequent performance.	Need to have enough participants to constitute four groups. Expensive to implement.

Figure 3.5. (Continued)

Internal and External Validity

The terms **internal validity** and **external validity** sometimes are used in connection with an evaluation's design. A design is internally valid if it enables the evaluator to be confident that a program is effective in a specific experimental instance. A design is externally valid if the evaluator can demonstrate that the program's results are applicable to participants in other places and at other times.

Internal validity is essential because, without it, the evaluator cannot tell whether a finding is due to the program or to some other factors or biases. For example, in an evaluation of a 5-year preventive health education program for high school students, the students may mature intellectually and emotionally, and this new maturity may be as important as the program in producing changes. This phenomenon is called *maturation*. In addition to maturation, internal validity includes other common risks:

♦ *History.* Historical events may occur that can bias the evaluation's results. For example, suppose a national campaign has been created to encourage young girls—a high-risk group—not to smoke. Suppose also that, during the course of the campaign, an influential television program relies on a heroine with an antismoking bias. In this case, the evaluator will have difficulty separating the effects of the campaign from the effects of the television program. In fact, the combination of the two may be required to affect smoking potential.

♦ *Instrumentation.* Unless the measures used to collect data are dependable, the evaluator cannot be sure the findings are accurate. For example, in a before-and-after design, an easier postmeasure than premeasure will erroneously favor the program. Untrained but lenient observers or test administrators can rule in favor of the program, while untrained but harsh observers or test administrators can rule against it.

♦ *Attrition.* Sometimes the participants who remain in the evaluation are different from those who drop out.

Risks to an evaluation design's external validity are most often the consequence of how participants are selected and assigned. For example, participants in an experimental evaluation can behave in atypical ways because they know they are in a special program; this is the Hawthorne effect. External validity is risked also when participants are tested, surveyed, or observed, because they may become alerted to the kinds of behaviors that are expected or favored.

The Evaluation Design Report: Questions, Standards, Independent Variables, and Designs

The evaluation design report (EDR) can be used in planning and explaining an evaluation. Designs begin with evaluation questions,

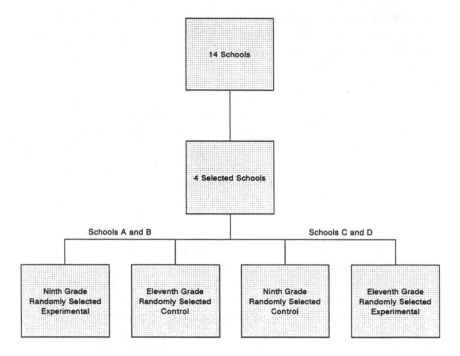

Figure 3.6. Evaluation Design for HAPPY: The Health Assessment and Prevention Program for Youth

standards, and independent variables, and the EDR depicts the relationship among them and the design.

The EDR in Figure 3.6 reports on the Health Assessment and Prevention Program for Youth (HAPPY), a school-based, teacher-delivered prevention curriculum to favorably modify health-related knowledge, beliefs, and self-confidence concerning health promotion and disease prevention among an eligible population of high school students from various racial and ethnic backgrounds in a large American city.

Boys and girls in the 9th and 11th grades in two pairs of demographically similar high schools are assigned to receive either a special six-lesson health promotion program (experiment) or no formal curriculum (control). The 4 schools are selected from the city's 14 academic high schools and were chosen on the basis of their combined representativeness (enrollment size and ethnic composition) of the total population of schools. A sample of 9th-grade classes in the first pair of schools and a sample of 11th-grade classes in the second pair constitutes the experimental group. The control groups are constituted from 9th- and 11th-grade classes in the corresponding schools.

Is this a true or a quasi experiment? HAPPY's design does not conform to the strictest definition of a randomized controlled trial because the two pairs of high schools were not selected at random. Once a school is selected, its participating classes, however, are chosen randomly.

Some evaluators will assert that the design is a randomized trial. It is clearly an experimental design with concurrent groups assigned randomly. Other evaluators will require more rigorous applications of experimental methodologies before calling HAPPY's evaluation design a true experiment.

The special curriculum—Health Assessment and Prevention Program for Youth (HAPPY)—focuses on conveying facts about healthful behaviors and risky ones and teaching skills necessary to practice good health habits. The main outcomes are measured by studying knowledge, beliefs, self-confidence, and behaviors. The measures take place just before the start of the curriculum and 3 months after its completion (see Figure 3.7).

A tabular representation of this design is shown in Figure 3.8.

Threats to Internal and External Validity:
HAPPY's Evaluation Design Limitations

HAPPY's evaluation design is not perfect. The external validity may be affected by the nonparticipation of eligible students in the premeasures of knowledge, beliefs, behaviors, and self-confidence. These students may have been absent or involved in some other school activity. Another threat to external validity is the unavailability of students for follow-up (primarily because of absenteeism). The

Evaluation Questions	Standards	Independent or Explanatory Variables	Evaluation Design
How effective is the program in favorably modifying knowledge, beliefs, self-confidence, and behaviors regarding health promotion and disease prevention?	A statistically and educationally significant improvement over a 3-month period for experimental students A statistically and educationally significant difference between experimental and control students	Group participation (experimental and control students)	An experimental design with concurrent controls and random assignment

Figure 3.7. Evaluation Design Report

	Experimental Group	Control Group
Grade 9	Schools A and B	Schools C and D
Grade 11	Schools C and D	Schools A and B

Figure 3.8. Experimental Evaluation Design With Randomly Assigned Concurrent Controls

evaluation findings may not apply to habitually absent students; these students, however, may have need for a preventive health care curriculum. Comparatively few schools are involved (4 of 14); the results may not apply to nonparticipants.

The internal validity of the evaluation may be compromised by the differential loss to follow-up across experimental and control groups. Also, students in the comparison group do not receive a standardized control program. Finally, much of the data may depend on students' responses (e.g., concerning their beliefs and self-confidence), and these may be of questionable validity.

Whether or not the potential limitations in HAPPY's design actually are present can be determined objectively. For example, students who do not participate can be compared with students who do on such variables as age, gender, ethnicity, health status (if available), and absenteeism. Students' responses to questions about their beliefs and self-confidence can be compared with those of other students who have participated in similar programs or who have used the same measure at other times. For example, if self-confidence is measured by a standardized and already validated measure, the obtained scores can be compared against these "norms."

SUMMARY AND TRANSITION TO NEXT CHAPTER ON SAMPLING

This chapter focused on ways to structure an evaluation so that program effects can be observed objectively. The structure includes the independent variables (e.g., the number and characteristics of the experimental and control groups) and number and timing of measures. The benefits and concerns associated with experimental and observational designs were discussed. A true experiment is advocated if the evaluator wants to establish causation, but this design is difficult to implement. Although not as rigorous, nonrandomized trials and observational designs are useful and used by evaluators. The next chapter discusses sampling: What to do when you cannot obtain the entire population for the evaluation. Among the issues discussed are how to obtain a random sample and how to select a large enough sample so that if program differences do exist, the evaluator will find them.

EXERCISE:
DESIGNING PROGRAM EVALUATIONS

Directions

Read the example below and give the evaluation questions, standards, independent variables, and design. Comment on the potential for bias or error in your choice of evaluation design.

The Center for Refugee Education wants to improve the quality of its education. Improved quality will be demonstrated by participants' improved reading ability and satisfaction with participation. Data will be collected from program participants and teachers immediately before and after the 2-year program.

Suggested Readings

Campbell, D. T., & Stanley, J. C. (1963). *Experimental and quasi-experimental designs for research.* Chicago: Rand McNally.

> The classic book on differing research designs. Threats to internal and external validity are described in detail. Issues pertaining to generalizability and how to get at "truth" are important reading.

Fink, A. (1993). *Evaluation fundamentals: Guiding health programs, research, and policy.* Newbury Park, CA: Sage.

> Discusses alternative evaluation designs and threats to internal and external validity.

Review Notes

Purpose of This Chapter

This chapter discusses the reasons for sampling and explains the advantages and limitations of commonly used methods. These include random, systematic, stratified, cluster, and convenience sampling. The chapter also discusses the issues to consider in deciding on an appropriate sample size. A form for reporting on the sampling strategy is examined. The report is designed to show the logical relationships among the evaluation questions, standards, independent variables, sampling strata, inclusion and exclusion criteria, dependent variables, measures, sampling methods, and size of the sample.

4 Sampling

What Is a Sample?

A sample is a portion or subset of a larger group called a population. The **target population** consists of the institutions, persons, problems, and systems to which or to whom the evaluation's findings are to be applied or "generalized." Consider the three target populations and samples in Example 4.1.

Example 4.1. Three Target Populations and Three Samples

1.
Target population: All homeless families throughout the United States

Program: Outreach; provision of education, housing, medical and financial assistance; and job training: The REACH-OUT Program

Sample: 500 homeless families in four states who spend at least 1 week in a shelter for families between April 1 and June 30

Comment: The REACH-OUT Program is designed for all homeless families. The evaluator plans to select a sample of 500 in four states between April 1 and June 30. The findings are to be applied to homeless families in all 50 states.

2.
Target population: All teacher training programs in the state

Program: Continuous Quality Improvement: An intervention to monitor and change the quality of teacher training. One index of quality is the performance of students on statewide reading and math tests.

Sample: Five teacher training institutions will be selected to try out the Continuous Quality Improvement experiment. After 1 year, for all participating teacher trainees, a 10% sample of student performance in reading and math will be taken.

Comment: The target for this evaluation is all teacher training programs in the state. Five will be selected for a Continuous Quality Improvement program. To appraise the program's quality, the evaluator will sample 10% of the students to assess their performance in reading and math. The findings are to be applied to all teacher training programs in the state.

3.
Target population: All students needing remediation in reading

Program: Options for Learning

Sample: Five schools in three counties; within each school, 15 classes; for each class, at least 20 students who need remediation in reading

Comment: Students who need assistance in reading are the targets of the program. The evaluators will select five schools in three counties, and within them, 15 classes with at least 20 students in each. The findings are to be applied to all students who need special aid in reading.

Inclusion and Exclusion Criteria

A sample is a constituent of a larger population to which the evaluation's findings will be applied. If an evaluator plans to investigate the impact of a counseling program on children's attitudes toward school, for example, and not all students in need of more favorable attitudes are to be included in the program, then the evaluator must decide on the types of students who will be the focus of the study. Will the evaluation concentrate on students of a specific age? with particular achievement levels? with poor attendance records? Example 4.2 contains hypothetical inclusion and exclusion criteria for an evaluation of such a program.

Example 4.2. Inclusion and Exclusion Criteria for a Sample of Students to Be Included in an Evaluation of a Program to Foster Favorable Attitudes Toward School

Inclusion

- ◆ All students attending schools in the zip codes listed below [not included in this example] who are currently in the sixth through ninth grades
- ◆ Must speak English or Spanish
- ◆ Must have participated in the E.T. (Eliminate Truancy) program

Exclusion

- ◆ All students who currently are incarcerated

The evaluator of this program has set criteria for the sample of students who will be included in the evaluation and for which conclusions will be appropriate. The sample will include children in the sixth through ninth grades who speak English and Spanish, who live within the confines of certain zip codes, and who have participated in the Eliminate Truancy (E.T.) program. The findings will not apply to students who meet only some of the criteria; for example, they are in the sixth grade, live in one of the specified zip codes, and speak Spanish, but have not participated in E.T.

The independent variables are the evaluator's guide to determining where to set inclusion and exclusion criteria. For example, suppose that, in an evaluation of the effects on teens of a preventive health care program, one of the questions asks whether boys and girls benefit equally from participation. In this evaluation question, the independent variable is gender and the dependent variable is benefit. If the evaluator plans to sample boys and girls, inclusion and exclusion criteria must be set. Hypothetical inclusion criteria could include boys and girls under the age of 18 who are likely to attend all of the educational activities for the duration of the evaluation and who have a reading level appropriate for their age or grade. Teens might be excluded if they already are participating in another preventive health care program, if they do not speak English, and if their parents object to their participation. If these hypothetical inclusion and exclusion criteria are used to guide sampling eligibility, then the evaluation's findings can be generalized only to English-speaking boys and girls under the age of 18 who read at grade level and who tend to be compliant with school attendance requirements. The findings are not designed to be applicable to teens who have difficulty reading or speaking English and who are unlikely to complete all program activities.

Methods of Sampling

Sampling methods usually are divided into two types. The first type, **probability sampling**, is considered the best way to ensure the validity of any inferences made about a program's effectiveness and its generalizability. In probability sampling, every member of the target population has a known probability of being included in the sample.

The second type is **convenience sampling**, in which participants are selected because they are available. In convenience sampling, some members of the target population have a chance of being chosen, while others do not. As a result, the data collected from a convenience sample may not be applicable to the target group at all. For example, suppose an evaluator of the student counseling service decided to interview all students who came for counseling during the week of December 26. Suppose also that 100 students came and that all agreed to be interviewed—a perfect response rate. The problem is that the end of December in some parts of the world is associated with respiratory viruses and skiing accidents; moreover, many schools are closed during that week and students are not around. Thus, the data collected by the happy evaluator with the perfect response rate could very well be biased because the evaluation excluded many students simply because they were not on campus (and, if they were ill, received care elsewhere).

SIMPLE RANDOM SAMPLING

In simple random sampling, every subject or unit has an equal chance of being selected. Because of this equality of opportunity, random samples are considered relatively unbiased. Typical ways of selecting a simple random sample include using a table of random numbers or a computer-generated list of random numbers and applying the numbers to lists of prospective participants.

Suppose an evaluator wanted to use a table and had the names of 20 teachers from which 10 were to be selected at random. First, the evaluator would assign a number, 1 to 20, to each name (e.g., Adams = 1, Baker = 2, Thomas = 20). This list of numbers is the **sampling frame**. Then, using a table of random numbers, which can be found in practically all statistics books, the evaluator would choose the first 10 digits between 1 and 20. Or, a list of 10 numbers between 1 and 20 can be generated by a computer. The next section illustrates the use of a table of random numbers in selecting a sample of 10 teachers from a list of 20.

One Way to Get a Random Sample:
Using a Table of Random Numbers

The evaluation team needed a randomly drawn sample of 10 teachers from a list of 20. Using a table of random numbers (see Figure 4.1), they first identified a row of numbers at random and then a column. Where the two intersected, the team began to identify their sample.

1. How they randomly identified the ROW. A member of the evaluation team tossed a die twice. The first die was 3; the second was 5. Starting with the first column, this corresponded to the third block and the fifth row of that block, expressed by the number 14575.

	Column 1	Column 2	Column 3	Column 4	Column 5	Column 6
Row 1	1 8 2 8 3	1 9 7 0 4[2]	4 5 3 8 7	2 3 4 7 6	1 2 3 2 3	3 4 8 6 5
	4 6 4 5 3	2 1 5 4 7	3 9 2 4 6	9 3 1 9 8	9 8 0 0 5	6 5 9 8 8
	1 9 0 7 6	2 3 4 5 3	3 2 7 6 0	2 7 1 6 6	7 5 0 3 2	9 9 9 4 5
	3 6 7 4 3	8 9 5 6 3	**1 2 3 7 8**	9 8 2 2 3	2 3 4 6 5	2 5 4 0 8
	2 2 1 2 5	1 9 7 8 6	2 3 4 9 8	7 6 5 7 5	7 6 4 3 5	6 3 4 4 2
Row 2	7 6 0 0 9	7 7 0 9 9	4 3 7 8 8	3 6 6 5 9	7 4 3 9 9	**0 3 4 3 2**
	0 9 8 7 8	7 6 5 4 9	8 8 8 7 7	2 6 5 8 7	4 4 6 3 3	7 7 6 5 9
	3 4 5 3 4	4 4 4 7 5	5 6 6 3 2	3 4 3 5 0	**0 1 7 6 8**	2 9 0 2 7
	8 3 1 0 9	7 5 8 9 9	3 4 8 7 7	2 1 3 5 7	2 4 3 0 0	0 0 8 6 9
	8 9 0 6 3	4 3 5 5 5	3 2 7 0 0	7 6 4 9 7	3 6 0 9 9	9 7 9 5 6
					9 4 6 5 6	3 4 6 8 9
Row 3	0 9 8 8 7	6 7 7 7 0	6 9 9 7 5	5 4 4 6 5	**1 3 8 9 6**	**0 4 6 4 5**
	2 3 2 8 0	3 4 5 7 2	9 9 4 4 3	9 8 7 6 5	3 4 9 7 8	4 2 8 8 0
	9 3 8 5 6	2 3 0 9 0	2 2 2 5 7	6 7 4 0 0	2 3 5 8 0	2 4 3 7 6
	2 1 2 5 6	5 0 8 6 3	5 6 9 3 4	7 0 9 9 3	3 4 7 6 5	3 0 9 9 6
	1 4 5 7 5[1]	3 5 4 9 0[3]	2 3 6 4 5	2 2 1 7 9	3 5 7 8 8	3 7 6 0 0
Row 4	2 3 2 7 6	7 0[4]8 7 0	**2 0 0 8 7**	6 6 6 6 5	7 8 8 7 6	5 8 0 0 7
	8 7 5 3 0	4 5 7 3 8	**0 9 9 9 8**	4 5 3 9 7	4 7 5 0 0	3 4 8 7 5
	0 0 7 9 1	3 2 1 6 4	9 7 6 6 5	2 7 5 8 9	9 0 0 8 7	**1 6 0 0 4**
	9 9 0 0 3	3 2 5 6 7	**0 2 8 7 8**	3 8 6 0 2	**1 8 7 0 0**	2 3 4 5 5
	1 4 3 6 7	6 4 9 9 9	7 8 4 5 3	4 0 0 7 8	5 3 7 2 7	2 8 7 5 9

[1] = Two rolls of a die yield 3 (3rd row) and 5 (5th number in the row, or 14575)
[2] = Two rolls of a die yield 2 (2nd column) and 1 (1st number in the row, or 19704)
[3] = Intersection of [1] and [2] (35490)
[4] = Go to next two-digit number to get the sample

Figure 4.1. A Portion of a Table of Random Numbers

NOTE: Numbers that are **boldface** = Sample of 10, consisting of numbers between 01 and 20

2. *How they randomly identified the COLUMN.* A member of the evaluation team tossed the die twice and got a 2 and a 1. This identified the second block of columns and the first block, represented by 19704. The starting point for this sample is immediately after the point at which the row 14575 and the column beginning with 19704 intersect, at 35490.

3. How the sample was chosen. The evaluation team needed 10 teachers from their list of 20—10 two-digit numbers. Moving down from 35490, the first 10 numbers between 01 and 20 that appear are 12, 20, 09, 02, 01, 13, 18, 03, 04, and 16. These are the teachers that comprise the random sample.

Random Selection and Random Assignment

In any given evaluation, random selection may be a different process from random assignment, as is illustrated in Example 4.3.

Example 4.3. Random Selection and Random Assignment: Two Examples

1. Evaluator A had 6 months to identify a sample of teens to participate in an evaluation of an innovative arts program. At the end of the 6 months, all eligible teens were assigned to the innovative or the traditional (control) program. The assignment was based on how close to a participating school each teen lived. This method was used because participation meant that students were required to attend several after-school activities, and no funding was available for transportation.

2. Evaluator B had 6 months to identify a sample of teens to participate in an evaluation of an innovative arts program. At the end of the 6 months, a sample was randomly selected from all who were eligible. Half the sample was randomly assigned to the innovative program and half to the traditional (control) program.

In the first situation, the evaluator selected all eligible teens and then assigned them to the experimental and control groups according to how close they lived to a participating school. In the second situation, the evaluator selected a random sample of all those who were eligible and then randomly assigned them to an experimental or control group. The second situation usually is considered preferable to the first. **Random selection** means that every eligible person has an equal chance; if all are included because they just happened to appear during the time allocated for sampling, biases may be introduced. Random assignment also can guard against bias.

SYSTEMATIC SAMPLING

Suppose an evaluator had a list of names of 3,000 high school seniors from which a sample of 500 was to be selected. In systematic sampling, 3,000 would be divided by 500 to yield six, and every sixth name would be selected. An alternative would be to select a number at random—say, by tossing a die. Suppose a toss came up with the number five. Then the 5th name would be selected first, then the 11th, 17th, and so on until 500 names were selected.

Systematic sampling should not be used if repetition is a natural component of the sampling frame. For example, if the frame is a list of names, those beginning with certain letters of the alphabet might get excluded because, for certain ethnicities, they appear infrequently.

STRATIFIED SAMPLING

A **stratified random sample** is one in which the population is divided into subgroups or "strata" and a random sample then is selected from each group. For example, in a program to teach students problem-solving skills, the evaluator might choose to sample students of differing ages, achievement (as indicated by scores on a 32-item test), and self-confidence (much = +; some = 0, and little = −). Age, achievement, and self-confidence are the strata. This sampling blueprint can be depicted as shown in Figure 4.2.

The strata or subgroups are chosen because the evaluator has evidence that they are related to the dependent variable or outcome measure—in this case, problem-solving skills; that is, the evaluator has evidence that general achievement, perceptions of self-confidence, and age influence ability to solve problems.

Achievement Scores and Self-Confidence	Age (Years)				
	5-6	7-9	10-12	13-15	16 or more
25-32 Points Much confidence					
Some					
Little					
17-24 Points Much confidence					
Some					
Little					
9-16 Points Much confidence					
Some					
Little					
1-8 Points Much confidence					
Some					
Little					

Figure 4.2. Sampling Blueprint for a Program to Teach Students Problem-Solving Skills

NOTE: Each "box" is called a **cell**. The cells in the sampling blueprint tell you the type of person that must be recruited for the sample. In this case, 60 cells must be filled. For instance, the very first cell (top left: first row, first column) must be filled with students who are 5 or 6 years old who scored between 25 and 32 points on the achievement test and have much confidence. The very last cell (bottom right: last row, last column) must be filled with students who are age 16 or older who scored between 1 and 8 points on the achievement test and have little confidence.

The justification for the selection of the strata must be evidence from the literature and other sources of information (e.g., historical data, expert opinion). If the evaluator neglects to use stratification in the choice of a sample, the final results may be confounded. For example, if the evaluation neglects to distinguish among women with different characteristics, good and poor performance may be averaged among them, and the program will seem to have no effect even if one or more groups benefited. In fact, the program actually might have been very successful with certain women—say, those over the age of 16, with achievement scores between 25 and 32, and with moderate self-confidence (Figure 4.2).

When stratification is not used, statistical techniques (e.g., analysis of covariance and regression) may be applied retrospectively (after the data have been collected) to correct for confounders or "covariates" on the dependent variables or outcomes. Evaluators generally agree, however, that it is better to anticipate confounding variables by sampling prospectively than to correct for them by analysis retrospectively. The reason is that statistical corrections require very strict assumptions about the nature of the data, assumptions for which the sampling plan may not have been designed. With few exceptions, using statistical corrections afterward results in a loss of power or ability to detect true differences between groups such as the experimental and control groups.

The strata are subsets of the independent variables. For example, if the independent variables are gender, achievement, and self-confidence, the strata are how each is defined. For example, gender is defined as male and female. A variable such as self-confidence can be defined in many ways, depending on the measures available to collect data and the needs of the evaluation. So, for example, it may be defined by a score on some standardized instrument or the results of students' judgment and classified as high, medium, or low, or excellent, very good, good, fair, or poor.

CLUSTER SAMPLING

Cluster sampling is used in large evaluations, those that involve many settings (e.g., schools, clinics, community-based service organizations, cities, states). In cluster sampling, the population is divided into batches. The batches can be randomly selected and assigned, and their constituents can be randomly selected and assigned. For example, suppose 10 counties are trying out a new program to improve reading levels; the control program is the traditional reading program. If you want to use random cluster sampling, you can consider each county to be a cluster and select and assign counties at random to the new or traditional programs. Alternatively, you can randomly select schools and randomly assign them to the experimental or the traditional program (assuming this were considered ethical).

Example 4.4 illustrates the use of cluster sampling in a survey of Italian parents' attitudes toward AIDS.

Example 4.4. Cluster Sampling and Attitudes of Italian Parents Toward AIDS

Social scientists from 14 of Italy's 21 regions surveyed parents of 725 students from 30 schools chosen by a cluster sample technique of the 292 classical, scientific, and technical high schools in Rome. Staff visited the schools and selected students by using a list of random numbers based on the school's size. Each of the selected students was given a letter, addressed to the parents, explaining the goals of the study and when they would be contacted.

NONPROBABILITY OR CONVENIENCE SAMPLES

Convenience samples are those for which the probability of selection is unknown. Evaluators use convenience samples simply because they are easy to get. This means that some people have no chance at all of being selected, simply because they are not around to be chosen. These samples are considered biased, or not representative of the target population, unless proven otherwise.

In some cases, statistical analyses can be performed to demonstrate that a convenience sample is really representative. For example, suppose that, during the months of July and August, an evaluator conducts a survey of parents regarding their views of the changes in the school district's dress code. Because those are months during which fortunate people try to get away and even take vacations, the respondents may be different from those who would answer the survey during the rest of the year. If the evaluator wants to demonstrate that the two samples (those who were around to respond and those who were not) are not different, the two groups can be compared on key variables such as income and education. These two variables may have an effect on who responds to the survey and on their responses. If no differences are found, then the evaluator is in a relatively stronger position to assert that even though the sample was chosen on the basis of convenience, its characteristics do not differ from the target population's on key variables.

The Sampling Unit

A major concern in sampling is the "unit" to be sampled. Consider Example 4.5.

Example 4.5. What Is the Target? Who Is Sampled?

An evaluation of the Teacher Instruction Program (TIP) aims to determine how effective it is in favorably modifying classroom teachers' instructional methods. The target population is all teachers who have taught continuously for 10 years or more. The evaluation question is "Have teachers favorably modified the diversity of their instruction?" The standards are that teachers in the experimental group show significant improvement over a 1-year period and significantly greater improvement than a control. Resources are available for 20 teachers to participate in the evaluation.

Ten teachers will be randomly assigned to the experimental group, and 10 will be assigned to the control. The evaluator plans to determine the effectiveness of the teachers' instructional methods by interviewing 10 students of each of the teachers in the experimental and control groups, for a total sample of 200 students. A consultant to the evaluation points out that even with 200 students, the evaluation is comparing the methods of 10 teachers against those of 10 teachers, and not the views on effectiveness of 100 students against that of 100 students. The reason is that characteristics of the instruction of any single teacher's students will be very highly related to one another. The consultant advises correcting for this lack of "independence among students of the same teacher" by using one of the statistical methods available for correcting for "cluster" effects. A contradictory consultant advises using a much larger number of students per teacher and suggests a statistical method for selecting the appropriate number. Because the evaluator does not have enough money to enlarge the sample, a decision is made to "correct" statistically for the dependence among students.

In the example, the evaluator wants to apply the evaluation's findings to all teachers but only has resources to include 20. In an ideal world, the evaluator would have access to a very large number of teachers. In this less-than-ideal world, however, the evaluator has resources to study 10 students per teacher and access to statistical methods to correct for possible biases. These statistical methods enable evaluators to provide remedies for the possible dependence among students who share a single teacher or teachers who teach in the same school, among mental health workers at a single clinic or the clients of a single worker, and so on.

Sample Size

POWER ANALYSIS AND ALPHA AND BETA ERRORS

An evaluation's ability to detect an effect is its power. A **power analysis** is a statistical method of identifying a sample size that is large enough to detect the effect, if one actually exists.

A commonly used evaluation research design is one in which two randomly assigned groups are compared to determine whether differences exist between them. "Does Program A differ from Program B in its ability to improve reading? math? art? mental health? social functioning?" is, accordingly, a typical evaluation question. To answer the question accurately, the evaluator must be sure that enough people are in each program group so that if a difference is actually present, it will be uncovered. Conversely, if there is no difference between the two groups, the evaluator does not want to conclude falsely that there is one. To begin the process of ensuring that the evaluation's sample size is adequate to detect any true differences, the first step is to reframe the appropriate evaluation questions into null hypotheses. **Null hypotheses** state that no difference exists between groups, as illustrated in Example 4.6.

Example 4.6. The Null Hypothesis in a Program to Improve Quality of Life

Question: Does Experimental Program A improve quality of life?

Standard: A statistically significant difference is found in quality of life between Experimental Program A's participants and Control Program B's. The difference is in Program A's favor.

Data source: The Quality of Learning Assessment, a 30-minute self-administered questionnaire with 100 questions. Scoring goes from 1 to 100, with 100 meaning excellent quality of life.

Null hypothesis: No difference in quality of learning exists for participants in Program A and in Program B (the mean scores obtained in Program A and in Program B are equal).

When an evaluator finds differences existing among programs and in reality there are no differences, that is an **alpha** or **Type I**

Truth

		Differences exist	No differences exist
Evaluator's conclusions from hypothesis test	Differences exist (Reject null)	Correct	Type I or alpha error
	No differences exist (Keep null)	Type II or beta error	Correct

Figure 4.3. Type I and Type II Errors: Searching for a True Difference

error. When an evaluator finds no differences among programs, though in reality there are differences, that is a **beta** or **Type II** error. The relationship between what the evaluator finds and the true situation can be depicted as shown in Figure 4.3.

Selecting a sample size that will maximize an evaluation's power relies on formulas whose use requires understanding hypothesis testing and having a basic knowledge of statistics. The formulas usually require the following:

♦ stating the null hypothesis
♦ setting a level (alpha or α) of statistical significance—usually .05 or .01—and deciding whether it is to be a one- or two-tailed test
♦ deciding on the smallest meaningful difference (e.g., the difference in mean scores between groups must be at least 15 points)
♦ setting the power $(1 - \beta)$ of the evaluation or the chance of detecting a difference (usually 80% or 90%)
♦ estimating the standard deviation (assuming that the distribution of the measure is normal) in the population

Alternative sample size calculations based on confidence intervals have been proposed. A confidence interval is computed from sample data that have a given probability that the unknown parameter (e.g., the mean) is contained within the interval. Common confidence intervals are 90%, 95%, and 99%.

Why Sample?

Evaluators sample because to do so is efficient and precise. Samples can be studied more quickly than target populations, and they are also less expensive to assemble. In some cases, recruiting a complete population for an evaluation is probably impossible even if time and financial resources are available. For example, enrolling all homeless families in an investigation of a program targeted to them is futile.

Sampling is also efficient; resources that might go into collecting data on an unnecessarily large number of individuals or groups can be spent on other evaluation activities, such as monitoring the quality of data collection and standardizing the implementation of the program.

Sampling enables the evaluator to focus on precisely the characteristics of interest. For example, suppose an evaluator wants to compare older and younger students with differing reading and math abilities. A stratified sampling strategy can give the evaluator just what is needed. A sample of the population with precise characteristics is more suitable for many evaluations than the entire population.

The Sampling Report

The sampling report (SR) can be used in planning and explaining an evaluation. The report contains the evaluation questions and standards, the independent variables, and strata, the evaluation design, inclusion and exclusion criteria, the dependent variable, the measure, the criteria for level of acceptable statistical and clinical (or educational or practical) significance, the sampling methods, and the size of the sample.

The following discussion illustrates the use of the SR for the Health Assessment and Prevention Program for Youth (HAPPY), a school-based, teacher-delivered prevention curriculum to favorably modify health-related knowledge, beliefs, and self-confidence concerning health promotion and disease prevention among an eligible population of high school students from various racial and ethnic backgrounds in a large American city. Standards of program effectiveness consist of sustained modifications in knowledge, beliefs, behavior, and self-confidence and significant differences between the experimental and control groups.

Boys and girls at or above grade level in reading in the 9th and 11th grades from two pairs of demographically similar high schools are assigned to receive either a special six-lesson health promotion program (experimental program) or no formal curriculum (control). Students with poor attendance records are excluded. The 4 schools are selected from the city's 14 academic high schools and are chosen on the basis of their combined representativeness (enrollment size and ethnic composition) of the total population of schools.

A 30% sample of 9th-grade classes (16 classes with 430 students) in the first members of the two pairs of schools is selected at random from the total 9th-grade enrollment to receive the experimental curriculum in the first semester. A 20% random sample of 9th-grade classes (10 classes totaling 251 students) in the second members of the two pairs serves as the comparison group (receives no formal preventive curriculum).

Similarly, a 30% sample of 11th-grade classes (13 classes totaling 309 students) in the second members of the two pairs of schools is selected at random from the total 11th-grade enrollment to receive the special prevention curriculum in the first semester, and a 20% random sample of the 11th-grade enrollment (13 classes with 326 students) in the first members of the two pairs serves as the control.

A total of 739 students are assigned to the experimental program and 577 to the control. A higher proportion of experimental than control students is sampled so that more students will be exposed to the special curriculum. The sampling strategy provides a greater than 80% power to detect a "small" treatment difference, holding a Type I error at 5%.

The sampling strategy for HAPPY can be illustrated graphically as in Table 4.1.

Looking at Table 4.2, you can see that the number of experimental classes is 16 + 13 (29) and that the number of experimental students is 430 + 309 (739). The number of control classes is 13 + 10 (23), and the number of control students is 326 + 251 (577).

The sampling report (SR) for HAPPY is given in Figure 4.4.

Table 4.1. How Sample Was Chosen From Four Schools: Two Pairs—AB and CD

	An Evaluation of HAPPY			
	Experimental		*Control*	
Schools	AB	CD	AB	CD
Grade	9	11	11	9
Semester	First	Second	Second	First
% Sample	30%	30%	20%	20%
# Classes	16	13	13	10
# Students	430	309	326	251

Table 4.2. HAPPY's Sample Size

	Experimental	*Control*
Classes	29	23
Students	739	577

SUMMARY AND TRANSITION TO NEXT CHAPTER ON COLLECTING INFORMATION

The next chapter discusses the issues involved in collecting data and describes and analyzes the sources of data available for evaluators. In the previous two chapters on evaluation design and sampling, the evaluator focused on the independent or predictor variables. These often consist of groups (e.g., experimental, control), demographics, and settings (e.g., classes, schools).

Associated with research design are the issues of sampling: Is sampling appropriate? Who should be sampled? How many people should be in each group? How will they be selected and assigned? Once these questions are answered, the evaluator shifts emphasis to data collection, the topic of the next two chapters.

In the next chapter, the sources of information available to the evaluator are discussed, as are their advantages and limitations. In evaluations, data are collected to describe participants, as well as to measure the effects of the program.

The Evaluation	The Report
Evaluation question	How effective is the program in favorably modifying knowledge, beliefs, self-confidence, and behaviors regarding health promotion and disease prevention?
Standard	A statistically and educationally significant improvement over a 3-month period for experimental students
	A statistically and educationally significant difference between experimental and control students
Evaluation design	An experimental design with concurrent controls and random assignment
Independent variables	Group participation (experimental and control students)
Strata	Group participation: experimental and control
Inclusion criteria	Must be in the 9th or 11th grade at the time of the study
	Must read English at or above grade level
Exclusion criteria	Poor attendance (two or more unexcused absences over the last month)
Dependent variable	Knowledge, beliefs, self-confidence, and behaviors
Measures	Knowledge: a 20-item achievement test; beliefs: a 25-item survey; self-confidence: an interview with 22 items; behaviors: a 30-item survey checklist
Criterion for educational meaning	Statistically significant findings on both standards. The level of significance is set at $p < .05$.
Sampling method	A 30% random sample of experimental classes (a cluster) and a 20% random sample of control classes

Figure 4.4. HAPPY's Sampling Report Form

EXERCISES: SAMPLING

1. Choose the sampling method used in each of the following situations.

Choices of Sample Method:

A. Simple random sampling

B. Stratified sampling

C. Cluster sampling

D. Systematic sampling

E. Convenience sampling

Situation	Choice *(Write in letter)*
1. The Rehabilitation Center has 40 separate family counseling groups, each with about 30 participants. The director of the center has noticed a decline in attendance rates and has decided to try an experimental program to improve them. The program is very expensive, and the center's directors can afford to finance only a 250-person program at first.	_____
Randomly selecting individuals from all group members will create friction and disturb the integrity of some of the groups. As an alternative, the evaluator has suggested a plan in which five of the groups—150 people—will be randomly selected to take part in the experimental program, and five will participate in the control.	
	continued

Situation	Choice (Write in letter)
2. The Medical Center has developed a new program to teach patients about cardiovascular fitness. The evaluation is determining how effective the program is with males and females of differing ages.	_____
The evaluation design is experimental with concurrent controls. In it, the new and traditional cardiovascular programs are compared. About 310 people signed up for the winter seminar. Of the 310, 140 are between ages 45 and 60, and 62 of these were men. The remaining 170 are between ages 61 and 75, and 80 of these are men. The evaluators randomly selected 40 persons from each of the four subgroups and randomly assigned every other person to the new program and the remainder to the old program.	
3. Two hundred health education teachers signed up for a continuing education program. Only 50, however, are to participate in an evaluation of the program's impact. Each participant is assigned a number from 001 to 200, and using a table, the evaluators select 50 names by reading down columns of three-digit random numbers and taking the first 50 numbers within the range of 001 to 200.	_____

Suggested Readings

Babbie, E. (1990). *Survey research methods.* Belmont, CA: Wadsworth.

> A basic survey research primer with an example of sampling in practice.

Baker, T. L. (1988). *Doing social research.* New York: McGraw-Hill.

> A how-to, with examples.

Burnam, M. A., & Koegel, P. (1988). Methodology for obtaining a representative sample of homeless persons: The Los Angeles skid row study. *Evaluation Review, 12,* 117-152.

> An excellent description of how to obtain a representative sample of an elusive population.

Campbell, D. T., & Stanley, J. C. (1963). *Experimental and quasi-experimental design for research.* Chicago: Rand McNally.

This is a classic book on the designs used to structure surveys and the research studies that include them. Because design and sampling interact, this is a valuable sourcebook.

Cook, D. C., & Campbell, D. T. (1979). *Quasi-experimentation: Design and analysis issues for field settings.* Boston: Houghton Mifflin.

This book discusses the issues that arise in fieldwork and quasi experimentation. It helps bring together issues that link design, sampling, and analysis.

Dillman, D. A. (1978). *Mail and telephone surveys: The total design method.* New York: John Wiley.

Reviews the special issues associated with mail and telephone surveys.

Frey, J. H. (1989). *Survey research by telephone.* Newbury Park, CA: Sage.

Contains a good review of the sampling questions that telephone surveys raise.

Henry, G. T. (1990). *Practical sampling.* Newbury Park, CA: Sage.

An excellent source of information about sampling methods and sampling errors. Although statistical knowledge helps, this book is worth reading even if the reader's knowledge is basic.

Kalton, G. (1983). *Introduction to survey sampling.* Beverly Hills, CA: Sage.

This excellent discussion of survey sampling requires understanding of statistics.

Kish, L. (1965). *Survey sampling.* New York: John Wiley.

This book is a classic and often is consulted in resolving issues that arise when actually implementing sampling designs.

Kraemer, H. C., & Thiemann, S. (1987). *How many subjects? Statistical power analysis in research.* Newbury Park, CA: Sage.

Although this book requires an understanding of statistics, the complexity of statistical power analysis is thoroughly discussed.

Lavrakas, P. (1987). *Telephone surveys.* Newbury Park, CA: Sage.

An important book for those interested in conducting a telephone survey.

Raj, D. (1972). *The design of sample surveys.* New York: McGraw-Hill.

Discusses the design and sampling issues associated with large surveys.

Rossi, P. H., Wright, S. D., Fisher, G. A., & Willis, G. (1987). The urban homeless: Estimating composition and size. *Science, 235,* 1336-1341.

A scholarly article on the difficulties of doing research with the urban homeless.

Stuart, A. (1984). *The ideas of sampling.* New York: Oxford University Press.

An interesting addition to a library for the statistically oriented who are interested in sampling issues.

Sudman, S. (1976). *Applied sampling.* New York: Academic Press.

Discusses issues pertaining to the conduct of large surveys and polls.

Review Notes

Purpose of This Chapter

This chapter covers the criteria for choosing among differing sources of evaluation information (including self-administered questionnaires, achievement tests, record reviews, observations, interviews, performance tests) and the literature and discusses their advantages and limitations. Special emphasis is given to reviewing the published literature for information because of the importance of reviews to competent evaluations. The next chapter covers how to evaluate the reliability and validity of existing measures of important health variables; the construction, selection, and coding of items and scales; and the preparation of a data collection plan.

5 Collecting Information

THE RIGHT DATA SOURCES

A Reader's Guide to Chapter 5

Information Sources: What's the Problem?

Choosing the Best Source of Data

Sources of Data and Their Advantages and
Limitations:
  Self-administered surveys, tests of achievement, record
  reviews, observations, interviews, performance tests, the
  literature

Information Sources: What's the Problem?

An evaluation team is studying the effectiveness of Health Assessment and Prevention Program for Youth (HAPPY), a school-based, teacher-delivered curriculum to favorably modify health-related knowledge, beliefs, and self-confidence concerning health promotion and disease prevention among an eligible population of high school students from various racial and ethnic backgrounds in a large American city.

Boys and girls in the 9th and 11th grades from two pairs of demographically similar high schools are assigned to receive either a special six-lesson health promotion program (experiment) or no formal curriculum (control). The 4 schools are selected from the city's 14 academic high schools and are chosen on the basis of their combined representativeness (enrollment size and ethnic composition) of the total population of schools. A sample of 9th-grade classes in the first pair of schools and a sample of 11th-grade classes in the second pair constitutes the experimental group. The control groups are constituted from 9th- and 11th-grade classes in the corresponding schools. Consider the illustrations from HAPPY's evaluation in Example 5.1.

Example 5.1. Evaluation Questions, Standards, Variables, and Data Sources

> *Evaluation Question 1:* How effective is the program in favorably modifying beliefs regarding health promotion and disease prevention?
>
> *Standard:* A statistically and educationally sustained improvement in beliefs that is statistically significantly different between experimental and control groups
>
> *Independent variable:* Group participation (experimental and control students)
>
> *Potential data sources:* School records for demographic data (e.g., age, ethnicity); interviews with parents and teachers to find out about the students' families and achievement
>
> *Dependent variable:* Beliefs

Potential data sources: Surveys of students, parents, and teachers

Comment: The characteristics of the experimental and control groups can be identified with data from surveys of the participants and reviews of their records. Information on beliefs can come from surveys of the students or of people who know them, such as parents and teachers.

Evaluation Question 2: How effective is the program in favorably modifying behaviors pertaining to health promotion and disease prevention?

Standard: A statistically and educationally sustained improvement in beliefs that is statistically significantly different between experimental and control groups

Independent variable: Group participation (experimental and control students)

Potential data sources: School records for demographic data (e.g., age, ethnicity); interviews with parents and teachers to find out about the students' families and achievement

Dependent variable: Behaviors

Potential data sources: Surveys of students to ask about behaviors; surveys of parents and teachers to ask about students' behaviors; observations of students; reviews of health and medical records

Comment: The characteristics of the experimental and control groups can be identified with data from surveys of the participants and reviews of their records. To find out about behaviors, sources of data include surveys, observations, and record review.

On what basis does the evaluator choose to interview the family or administer a questionnaire to the study's participants? How does the evaluator decide between record reviews and surveys? Answering these questions is at the heart of a program evaluation's data collection.

Choosing the Best Source of Data

Evaluators have access to an arsenal of information collection sources. Among them are self-administered questionnaires, tests of performance and achievement, face-to-face and telephone interviews, observations, the literature, and personal, financial, and other records. Each has its advantages and limitations. To choose a source of data, use the following guidelines to ask questions.

Guidelines for Questions to Ask in Choosing a Data Source

♦ What variables need to be measured? Are they defined and specific enough to measure?

♦ Can you borrow or adapt a currently available measure, or must a new measure be created?

♦ If an available measure seems to be appropriate, has it been tried out in circumstances that are similar to the present evaluation's?

♦ Do you have the technical skills, financial resources, and time to create a valid measure?

♦ If no measure is available or appropriate, can you develop one in the time allocated for the evaluation?

♦ Do you have the technical skills, financial resources, and time to collect information with the chosen measure?

♦ Are participants likely to be able to fill out forms, answer questions, and provide information called for by the measure?

♦ In studies that involve use of information from school and other confidential records, can you obtain permission to collect data in an ethical way?

♦ To what extent will users of the evaluation's results (e.g., teachers, parents, students, patients, program developers, sponsors) have confidence in the sources of information on which they are based?

Example 5.2 shows what can happen when evaluators neglect to answer these questions.

Example 5.2. (Not) Collecting Evaluation Information: A Case Study

The evaluators of an innovative high school science curriculum were concerned with getting students interested in pursuing biomedical careers. A major component of the curriculum consisted of teaching the students about human blood transfusion, knowledge needed to work in clinical laboratories. The evaluators prepared a written test of achievement and included questions about the consequences of transfusing incompatible red cells, what to do about RH negative females who may bear children, and what to do when no compatible blood is available. The test was given immediately before and within 1 month after the students completed the curriculum.

The evaluators also prepared a measure of students' understanding of ethical issues involved in blood transfusion. The measure consisted of 10 fictitious scenarios with ethical components, and the idea was to compare students' responses with those given by students in a similar program in another college.

Finally, the evaluators planned to distribute a self-administered survey to students to determine whether their attitudes toward careers in the clinical laboratory sciences changed for the better as a result of their exposure to the curriculum.

The results of the evaluators' activities were to be presented at a special meeting of the School's Board of Trustees after the first year of the curriculum.

The evaluators' report was very brief. Although they were able to locate a number of achievement tests for high school students with questions about blood transfusions and thus did not have to prepare them from scratch, they could not find an appropriate time to give all students a premeasure and a postmeasure. This meant that the evaluators had incomplete information on the performance of many students, with only pretests for some and only posttests for others. In addition, the evaluators found that developing the scenarios took about 9 months because they were more difficult to compile than had been anticipated. A sample of students were enlisted to try out the scenarios, and they found the questions ambiguous and hard to understand. The evaluators had to rewrite and retest the scenarios, which were not even ready for use at reporting time. Finally, many students refused to complete the attitude questionnaire. Anecdotal information suggested the students thought that they were overloaded with tests and questionnaires and that these additional ones did not seem to be important. Because of the poor quality of the data, the evaluators were unable to provide any meaningful information about the curriculum.

In the case study just presented, the evaluators encountered difficulties for the following reasons:

+ not enough time to collect data on students' achievement before and after
+ not enough time and possibly insufficient skills to prepare the scenarios
+ choice of information collection method that was not appropriate for the participants because they were unwilling to complete it

Sources of Data and
Their Advantages and Limitations

The following sections describe the characteristics, advantages, and limitations of seven of the most commonly used sources of data in evaluations.

1. SELF-ADMINISTERED SURVEYS

Self-administered surveys (also called "questionnaires") ask individuals to answer questions or items. The answers typically are

During the past 4 weeks, have you had any of the following problems studying or doing your routine activities (e.g., sports or even just hanging out) as a result of any emotional problems (e.g., feeling depressed or anxious)? Answer YES or NO for each question by circling 1 or 2 on each line.

	Yes	No
Cut down the amount of time you spent on studying or other activities?	1	2
Accomplished less than you would like?	1	2
Didn't study or do other activities as usual?	1	2

Figure 5.1. Self-Administered Survey Item

recorded directly on the survey. A typical survey item might look like the one presented in Figure 5.1.

Advantages

♦ Many people are accustomed to completing surveys.

♦ Many surveys and rating scales are available for adaptation.

♦ Self-administered surveys are conducive to confidentiality and anonymity.

♦ Surveys can be administered to large groups of people at relatively low cost.

Disadvantages

♦ The people who respond (called the "respondents") may not always tell the truth.

♦ The self-administered survey's format is not suitable for obtaining explanations of behavior or sensitive information.

♦ Without supervision, some respondents may fail to answer some or even all questions.

2. TESTS OF ACHIEVEMENT

The most commonly used method of collecting information on educational accomplishment is the written achievement test. Written tests tend to measure knowledge, understanding, and application of theories, principles, and facts. To assess higher levels of learning, such as the evaluation of evidence or the synthesis of information from varying sources, other methods, such as observation of performance or analysis of written papers and scientific studies, are more appropriate.

Most evaluations of educational programs rely to some extent on written tests of achievement, and many of these are multiple choice, as shown in Example 5.3.

Example 5.3. Multiple-Choice Question on an Achievement Test

For an evaluation of a course in program evaluation, what is the best source of data on whether or not students have learned basic facts? **Circle one choice only**.

The literature	1
Achievement tests	2
Record reviews	3
Performance tests	4

---

3. RECORD REVIEWS

Record reviews are used in educational evaluations to obtain information on student performance, attendance, and demographics.

Reasons for Coming to the Room		
Why did the client come to the Room? Mark yes OR no to each.		
	1. Yes	2. No
Creative Workshops		
Gymnastics/sports	1	2
Dance	1	2
Martial arts	1	2
Arts/crafts	1	2
Vocational	1	2
Performing arts	1	2
Health Concerns		
Family planning	1	2
Medical services	1	2
Health counseling	1	2
Perinatal services	1	2
Pregnancy evaluation/counseling	1	2
Learning/Career		
Career counseling/education-vocational skills training	1	2
ESL	1	2
GED	1	2
Learning center	1	2
School credit	1	2
Legal Services	1	2
Meal/Food Service	1	2

Figure 5.2. Portion of a Record Review Form: Evaluating the Room—A Program for Teens

They can be used also to obtain data on school finances, staffing patterns, and so on. Record reviews are used frequently in social programs to keep track of people in the system and to monitor the number and type of services they use. Figure 5.2 is a component of a record review system to evaluate a program called the Room. This program aims to provide consolidated services for adolescents in a single-service service center.

Advantages

♦ Collecting data from records can be relatively unobtrusive in that office and school procedures need not be disturbed.

♦ If you need data on quantity (e.g., number of absences, types of classes taken or services used), this is an excellent source.

♦ If data are needed on some demographics (e.g., age, gender), records are an accurate source.

Disadvantages

♦ Finding information in the record can make this a time-consuming activity.

♦ You must be sure the review process is reliable and accurate. This may mean training people to do the abstractions (and training is time-consuming and expensive) or developing and validating review forms.

♦ Certain types of information are not in all records (e.g., behavior problems, special activities or problems).

4. OBSERVATIONS

Observations are appropriate for describing the environment (e.g., the size of a classroom, how it is furnished) and for obtaining global portraits of the dynamics of a situation (e.g., a typical problem-solving session in a social studies class, a "day in the life" of a school). A portion of an observation form is shown in Figure 5.3.

Advantages

♦ Observations provide an opportunity to collect firsthand information.

♦ They can provide information that cannot be anticipated.

	Circle one
Are the exits clearly marked?	
Yes, all areas	1
Yes, some areas	2
No, no areas	3
Do the windows have draperies or blinds?	
Yes	1
No	2
Not applicable because no windows	3

Figure 5.3. Portion of an Observation Form

Disadvantages

♦ A structured format and extensive training are required for depend able observations.

♦ Observations are labor-intensive and time-consuming.

♦ The observer can influence the environment being studied, and people can act different from usual because they are being "watched."

5. INTERVIEWS

Interviews can be conducted in person and on the telephone. Figure 5.4 is an excerpt from a face-to-face interview with students in Health Assessment and Prevention Program for Youth (HAPPY), a high school program to improve health knowledge, behaviors, and self-confidence.

Advantages

♦ It allows individuals to ask about the meaning of questions.

♦ Information can be collected from people who may have difficulty reading or seeing.

9. **ASK**: Have you ever been told by a doctor, nurse, or other health care professional that you are overweight?

        [ ] No: **GO TO QUESTION 10**
        [ ] Yes: **CONTINUE**

9a. **ASK**: How long ago were you told that you were overweight? (**Read list to student. SAY**: Before you answer, I will read you a list.)

        [ ] Less than 1 year ago
        [ ] About 1 year ago
        [ ] More than 1 year ago

9b. **ASK**: Since you were told you were overweight, which of the following did you do? (**SAY**: Before you answer, I will read you a list.)

        [ ] I went on a weight-reducing diet.
        [ ] I became more serious about an exercise program.
        [ ] I changed the type of food I eat.
        [ ] I stopped smoking.
        [ ] I didn't do anything special.

Figure 5.4. Portion of an Interview

Disadvantages

- ♦ Interviews are time-consuming and labor-intensive.
- ♦ Interviewers require extensive training and monitoring.
- ♦ Special skills may be required to interpret responses that are "off-the-record."

6. PERFORMANCE TESTS

Performance tests are a type of observational measure in which participants are asked to complete a task or to make something. Then the evaluator assesses the quality of the performance or product. For instance, a performance test can be used to appraise students' ability

	Circle one	
Essential		
Makes referral to psychosocial counseling line	Yes	No
Acceptable		
Makes referral to other mental health facility (name:)	Yes	No
Unacceptable		
Volunteer counsels caller	Yes	No
Call terminated by volunteer	Yes	No

Answer **each** of the following questions.

	Mark yes **or** no for each question.	
	1. Yes	2. No
Was the information disclaimer used?	1	2
Was the referral disclaimer used?	1	2
Did the volunteer offer to send written material?	1	2

Please rate the volunteers' empathy and the clarity of information. **Mark one choice for each.**

	1. Excellent	2. Very Good	3. Good	4. Fair	5. Poor	9. Unable to Observe
Clarity						
Empathy						

Figure 5.5. Portions of a Form to Assess a Test of Performance

to bake a pie, prepare a slide for a microscope, or conduct a telephone interview. Figure 5.5 is an excerpt from a form used to assess the quality of interviews with the public conducted by volunteers at a cancer hot line.

Advantages

+ A performance test is useful in measuring specific skills.
+ It provides the learner with a virtual-reality situation to practice and learn.

Disadvantages

+ A performance test is applicable to a limited number of school-based types of learning.
+ It requires agreed-on criteria of performance.
+ Such a test requires trained observers or scores to ensure a fair appraisal of performance.
+ Because of limited applicability, it can be expensive to implement the test and interpret the results.

7. THE LITERATURE

Evaluators use the literature for reasons as diverse as gathering ideas for research designs and data collection and analysis methods and comparing data and conclusions across research. The term **literature** means published and unpublished reports of studies or statistical findings. Published reports are often easier to locate (because they are in books and journals accessible to libraries). Because they have the advantage of public scrutiny, their methods (and conclusions) may be more dependable than unpublished findings. Publication may be in a scholarly journal, a book, or a report or monograph produced by local, state, or national agencies. Following are guidelines for using the literature in program evaluation.

Guidelines for Using the Literature
in Program Evaluation

1. *To set standards.* The literature can provide information on the past performance of programs and populations. These may serve as a yardstick in planning an evaluation and in comparing the findings of one that already has been completed.

2. *To define variables.* The literature is a primary source of information about the ways others have defined and measured commonly used variables in education and psychology, including achievement, development, child abuse and neglect, counseling, and disability.

3. *To determine sample size.* Power calculations to arrive at sample sizes large enough to reveal true differences (if they exist) require an estimation of the variance—a measure of dispersion—in the sample or population. Sometimes, however, evaluators have no readily available data on the variance in the sample of interest. The evaluator can conduct a pilot study to obtain the data. Appropriate data may be available in the literature, however, enabling the evaluator to build on and expand the work of others.

4. *To obtain examples of designs, measures, and ways of analyzing and presenting data.* The literature can be used as a source for obtaining sound information on research methods and data collection, analysis, and reporting techniques.

5. *To determine the significance of the evaluation and of its findings.* The literature often is used to justify the need for the program and for the evaluation questions. It also is used to show whether the evaluation's findings confirm or contradict the results of other studies and to identify areas in which little or no knowledge is currently available.

6. *To conduct meta-analyses.* Meta-analyses are techniques for pooling the results of true experiments. The idea is to combine the results of smaller, more local studies to increase the power of the findings. Because not all experiments are of equal quality, understanding how to review and interpret the literature is an important first step in conducting a meta-analysis. Very few program evaluations are ran-

domized, controlled trials, and so this technique has not been used often. Evaluations are becoming more sophisticated, so perhaps meta-analyses will be more appropriate and common in the near future.

The following sections constitute a six-step guide to reviewing the literature.

A Six-Step Guide for Reviewing the Literature

1. *Assembling the Literature.* The key to an efficient search through the literature is specificity. If you want all evaluations published in English by Jones between 1980 and 1993 about evaluations of U.S. elementary school reading programs, you are much more likely to get what you want than if you ask for all published evaluations of reading programs in U.S. schools. If Jones has published articles about evaluations in U.S. elementary schools that have appeared in the education, psychology, or social science literature, then certain articles may not turn up if you rely solely on a computerized search of one database. For a more comprehensive search, you should investigate all potentially relevant databases, scrutinize the references in key articles, and ask experts in the field to recommend references and bibliographic databases.

The search itself requires careful specification of the variables and populations of concern. A first step is to decide on specific criteria for a study's inclusion into and exclusion from the literature review. Once these criteria are established, the terms used to describe them can be employed to guide the search. These are called "search terms."

2. *Identifying Inclusion and Exclusion Criteria.* Inclusion and exclusion criteria are used for deciding whether a study is appropriate or inappropriate for review. They usually include attention to the variables and populations of concern, where and when the study was published, and its methodological quality, as can be seen in Example 5.4, an example of the inclusion and exclusion criteria for a review of the effectiveness of mental health services for very young mothers (age 16 and younger) in prenatal care programs.

Example 5.4. Illustrative Inclusion and Exclusion Criteria for a Review of Evaluated Programs to Improve the Mental Health of Very Young Mothers

We included evaluations of programs aiming to integrate medical and social services to improve the mental health outcomes of very young mothers. We selected only published evaluations because the editorial review process screens out the poorest studies. We chose 1985 as a starting point so that we would have a decade's data reflecting the increased accessibility of integrated services begun by the United States government in the 1960s and 1970s. We excluded research that focused on the organization of health services (e.g., centralizing a region's mental health services).

With these inclusion and exclusion criteria as guides, the evaluator can focus on a search for studies published from 1985 forward and in all languages. The search terms probably will include program evaluation, mental health services and outcomes, and adolescent health care.

Example 5.5 shows the terms that were used to search the literature to find out about programs to care for people with post-traumatic stress disorder (PTSD) (including victims of rape, combat veterans, torture victims, and the tragically bereaved).

Example 5.5. Search Terms for Electronic Bibliographic Databases

Post-traumatic stress disorder: traumatic stress, treatment, psychotherapy, flooding, PTSD, behavior therapy, pharmacotherapy, drugs, and cognitive therapy

3. *Selecting Literature.* After the articles are assembled, they invariably need to be screened for irrelevant material. Because few searches (and searchers) are perfect, studies invariably are obtained that do not address the topic or that are methodologically unsound.

Screens often consist of methodological criteria. For example, articles may be screened out because they do not have a control group, data come from unreliable sources, insufficient data are presented on some important variable, or the study's findings are preliminary.

4. *Identifying the "Best" Literature.* Regardless of the scope of the literature review, a method must be employed that distinguishes among articles with differing levels of quality. Selecting the best literature means finding the most methodologically rigorous studies.

At least two individuals are needed to make an adequate appraisal of a study's quality. These individuals should be given a definition of the parameters of quality and trained to use them. Before the formal review, they should test their understanding of the system by collaborating on 1 to 10 articles. A third knowledgeable person can act as adjudicator in cases of disagreement.

Figure 5.6 is an example of a set of methodologic features and definitions that were used to appraise the quality of the published program evaluation literature.

The evaluator can decide that, to be categorized as "best," a study must meet all of the criteria or some fraction (a score of more than 5 of 8) or achieve certain minimum criteria (e.g., random

---

Criteria for Selecting the Best

Description of the experimental program is clear (data were given on program's duration, funding level, teachers, students, standardization across sites, etc.).

Participants are randomly selected into the evaluation (all eligible participants were selected or a random sampling).

Participants are randomly assigned to groups.

Data are collected prospectively.

Data collected for the evaluation are demonstrated to be valid for all main variables.

Evaluation focuses on outcomes (e.g., ability to read, write, compute; job performance)

Evaluation collects more than one measurement after participants complete the program.

Statistical information is sufficient to determine educational and practical significance of the findings.

Figure 5.6. Rating Methodologic Features of the Literature: Identifying the Best Published Program Evaluation

assignment and valid data collection). Needless to say, these choices are somewhat arbitrary, and their merits must be defended on a case-by-case basis.

An important component of the process of deciding on a study's quality is agreement among reviewers. To identify the extent of agreement, each item in the review can be examined independently or reviewers' scores on the entire set of items can be compared.

When two or more persons measure the same item and their measurements are compared, an index of interrater reliability is obtained. One statistic often used in deciding on the degree of agreement between two reviewers on a dichotomous variable (valid data were collected: yes or no) is *kappa* (κ). The statistic used to

SECTION IV: Methods (continued)

Data Sources:

A. Methods:
(Check all that apply)

[ ] Direct observation   [ ] Self-administered questionnaire
[ ] Telephone survey   [ ] Face-to-face interview
[ ] Literature review   [ ] Other, specify:_____

B. Variables measured:
(Check all that apply)

[ ] Age
[ ] Race/ethnicity
[ ] Reading ability
[ ] Mathematics ability
[ ] Psychosocial attributes (e.g., self-esteem)
　　If yes, specify all:

continued

Figure 5.7. Excerpts From a Form for Obtaining Information on a Study's Data Collection

examine the relationship between two numerical characteristics (Reviewer A's score of 5 vs. Reviewer B's score of 7 points) is *correlation.*

Not all literature reviews are done by two or more persons. Then, intrarater reliability can be calculated by using kappa or correlation. To do this, a single reviewer should rate or score a selection of articles at least twice and compare the results.

5. *Abstracting Information.* The most efficient way to obtain data from the literature is to standardize the abstraction process. A uniform abstraction system guards against the possibility that some important information will be missed, ignored, or misinterpreted. To obtain information on a study's data collection, a form like the one in Figure 5.7 is useful.

C. Reliability/Validity:

1. Is any information regarding the **reliability** of selected forms, surveys, or other data collection methods discussed?
[ ] YES → If YES, specify (e.g., Cronbach's alpha, Kuder-Richardson, etc.): _____
[ ] NO/CANNOT TELL

2. Is any information regarding the **validity** of study design, data collection, or findings discussed?
[ ] YES → If YES, specify (e.g., used previously validated forms, reported validation studies, etc.): _____
[ ] NO/CANNOT TELL

3. Are data collection procedures **standardized**? (Check all that apply)
[ ] YES
[ ] NO/CANNOT TELL

D. Duration of Data Collection Period: ___ ___ months
(Convert all periods to months and sum if > 1 period)
Years of Data Collection Period: 19 ___ ___ to 19 ___ ___

Figure 5.7. (Continued)

Suppose you wanted to abstract information on the characteristics of the programs that were being evaluated. You might collect information by using a form like the one shown in Figure 5.8.

6. *Unpublished Literature and Negative Results: What Gems Are in the File?* Various analyses of the published literature have suggested the existence of a bias in favor of positive results. This means that if a review is based solely on published articles, negative findings may be underrepresented. Finding unpublished articles (in someone's "file drawer"), however, is not an easy task. Published studies have been reviewed by experts, peers, and colleagues, and the most unreliable probably have been screened out. Nevertheless, when interpreting the findings from the published literature, the evaluator should consider the potential biases that may exist because unpublished articles are excluded.

Programs

Program/Site   [ ] One program, one site (GO TO **A**)
combinations: [ ] One program, several sites (GO TO **B**)
(Check one)   [ ] Multifaceted program, one site (GO TO **C**)
                        [ ] Multifaceted program, several sites (GO TO **D**)

A. ONE PROGRAM/ONE SITE:

  1. Program adequately described?

     [ ] YES → If **YES,** provide brief synopsis of program description:

     _____

     _____

     _____

     [ ] NO

  2. Duration of program: ____ ____ months
     (Enter '99' if unknown or not reported)
     (e.g., convert 3 years to 36 months)

  3. Funding level (in U.S. dollars)
     (Check one)
     [ ] Not stated   [ ] $500,000 to < $1 million
     [ ] < $50,000   [ ] $1 million to < $2 million
     [ ] $50,000 to < $100,000   [ ] $2 million to < $5 million
     [ ] $100,000 to < $250,000   [ ] ≥ $5 million
     [ ] $250,000 to < $500,000

continued

Figure 5.8. Portions of a Form to Abstract Information on the Characteristics of a Program Being Evaluated

B. ONE PROGRAM/SEVERAL SITES:

1. Program adequately described?

   [ ] YES → If **YES,** provide brief synopsis of program description:

   _____

   _____

   _____

   [ ] NO

2. Duration of program: ____ ____ months
   (Enter '99' if unknown or not reported)
   (e.g., convert 3 years to 36 months)

3. Funding level: (Check one)
   [ ] Not stated   [ ] $500,000 to < $1 million
   [ ] < $50,000   [ ] $1 million to < $2 million
   [ ] $50,000 to < $100,000   [ ] $2 million to < $5 million
   [ ] $100,000 to < $250,000   [ ] ≥ $5 million
   [ ] $250,000 to < $500,000

4. Number of sites: ____ ____   [ ] CHECK HERE IF THERE
                                      ARE 100 OR MORE SITES

5. Is the program standardized across sites?
   [ ] YES   [ ] NO   [ ] DON'T KNOW

Figure 5.8. (Continued)

SUMMARY AND TRANSITION TO NEXT CHAPTER
ON EVALUATION MEASURES

This chapter explained the factors that should be taken into account when deciding on a measure or source of data for an evaluation. First, the evaluation question must be reviewed carefully so that all variables are known and clarified. Second, the evaluator should consider the possible measures that are likely to provide information on each variable. Among the possibilities are self-administered questionnaires, tests of achievement and performance, record reviews, observations, and interviews. Each has advantages and limitations. For example, interviews enable the evaluator to question program participants in a relatively in-depth manner, but they can be time-consuming and financially costly. Self-administered questionnaires may be less time-consuming and costly, but they lack the intimacy of interviews; also, the evaluator must always worry about the rate of responses. In selecting a source of data, look first at the evaluation question, decide whether you have the technical and financial resources and the time to develop your own measure; if not, you must consider adopting or adapting an already-existing measure. You must consider also the credibility to participants and consumers of whatever data source you choose. Remember to consult the literature whenever possible to identify what is available and where the present evaluation fits into the larger scheme of things.

The next chapter discusses reliability and validity. Reliability refers to the consistency of the information from each source; validity refers to its accuracy. The chapter also discusses the steps required in developing and validating your own measure, as well as in outlining the activities involved in selecting a measure that has been developed by other evaluators. Among the issues reviewed in the next chapter is coding—that is, making sure your measure is properly formatted or described from the point of view of the person who will enter the data into the computer. Another important issue is making sure the components of the evaluation are linked logically. The measurement chart helps portray the logical connections among the evaluation's variables and measures.

EXERCISE: COLLECTING INFORMATION: THE RIGHT DATA SOURCES

Directions

Match the descriptions and measures.

Descriptions	Measures
1. May alter the experimental environment	A. Self-administered surveys
2. Relatively inexpensive but may not get responses to all questions	B. Record reviews
3. May measure what you know but does not measure what you can do	C. Literature
4. Not intrusive but may not contain much psychosocial information	D. Achievement tests
5. Particularly useful in the standard-setting process	E. Observations

Suggested Readings

Kosecoff, J., & Fink, A. (1982). *Evaluation basics.* Newbury Park, CA: Sage.

Contains descriptions of various sources of data used in evaluations of programs in health, education, and social welfare. Gives rules for writing multiple-choice and other types of questions.

Solomon, S. D., Gerrity, E. T., & Muff, A. M. (1992). Efficacy of treatments for post-traumatic disorder: An empirical review. *Journal of the American Medical Association, 268,* 633-638.

Provides a useful way of summarizing the results of literature reviews that are not appropriate for meta-analyses.

Purpose of This Chapter

This chapter starts with the concepts of reliability and validity. **Reliability** refers to the consistency of a measure; **validity** refers to its accuracy. Reliable and valid measures are the key to a sound evaluation because they are indicators of the quality on which findings and conclusions are based. This chapter also discusses how to develop and select valid measures, prepare a coding strip for data entry, and use a measurement chart to establish logical connections among the evaluation's questions and design and measures.

Evaluation Measures

E valuators sometimes create their own measures, and sometimes they adapt or adopt parts or all of already-existing ones. Because the conclusions of an evaluation are based on data from these measures, their quality must be demonstrably high for the evaluation's results to be sound (otherwise, we have the well-known phenomenon of "garbage-in-garbage-out"). Determining the quality of the data collection measures means understanding their reliability and validity.

Reliability

A reliable measure is relatively free from "measurement error." Because of this "error," individuals' obtained scores are different from their true scores (which can be obtained only from perfect measures). What causes this error? In some cases, the error results from the measure itself: It may be difficult to understand or poorly administered. For example, a self-administered questionnaire regarding the value of a college education might produce unreliable results if its reading level is too high for the teens who are to complete it. If the reading level is on target but the directions are unclear, the measure will be unreliable. Of course, the evaluator could simplify the language and clarify the directions and still find measurement error. This is because measurement error also can come directly from the examinees. For example, if teens are asked to complete a questionnaire and they are especially anxious or fatigued, their obtained scores could differ from their true scores.

In program evaluation, four kinds of reliability often are discussed: stability, equivalence, homogeneity, and interrater and intrarater reliability.

STABILITY

Stability sometimes is called "test-retest reliability." A measure is stable if the correlation between scores from time to time is high. Suppose a survey of students' attitudes was administered to the same group of students at School A in April and again in October.

142

If the survey was reliable and no special program or intervention was introduced, on average, we would expect attitudes to remain the same. The major conceptual difficulty in establishing test-retest reliability is in determining how much time is permissible between the first and second administrations. If too much time elapses, external events might influence responses for the second administration; if too little time elapses, the respondents may remember and simply repeat their answers from the first administration.

EQUIVALENCE

Equivalence, or **alternate-form reliability**, refers to the extent to which two assessments measure the same concepts at the same level of difficulty. Suppose students were given an achievement test before participating in a new computer skills class and then again 2 months after completing it. Unless the evaluator was certain the two tests were of equal difficulty, better performance after the second administration could represent performance on an easier test, rather than improved learning. Moreover, because this approach to reliability requires two administrations, a problem may arise concerning the appropriate interval between them.

As an alternative to establishing equivalence between two forms of the same instrument, evaluators sometimes compute a split-half reliability. To do this requires dividing an instrument into two equal halves (or alternate forms) and obtaining the correlation between the two halves. Problems arise if the two halves vary in difficulty; however, because only one administration is required, at least the concern about the duration of intervals between testing is eliminated.

HOMOGENEITY

Homogeneity refers to the extent to which all items or questions assess the same skill, characteristic, or quality. Sometimes this type of reliability is referred to as "internal consistency." A Cronbach's coefficient alpha (basically, the average of all correlations between each item and the total score) often is calculated to determine the extent of homogeneity. For example, suppose an evaluator created a questionnaire to determine students' satisfaction with Textbook A. An analysis of homogeneity will tell the extent to which all items on the questionnaire focus on satisfaction.

Some variables do not have a single dimension. Student satisfaction, for example, may consist of satisfaction with school in general, their school in particular, teachers, classes, extracurricular activities, and so on. If an evaluator is unsure of the number of dimensions included in an instrument, a factor analysis can be performed. This statistical procedure identifies "factors" or relationships among the items or questions.

INTERRATER AND INTRARATER RELIABILITY

Interrater reliability refers to the extent to which two or more individuals agree. Suppose two individuals were sent to a school to observe the appearance of offices and classrooms and the general atmosphere. If the observers agreed perfectly on all items, then interrater reliability would be perfect. Interrater reliability is enhanced by training data collectors, providing them with a guide for recording their observations, monitoring the quality of the data collection over time to see that people are not "burning out," and offering a chance to discuss difficult issues or problems. **Intrarater reliability** refers to a single individual's consistency of measurement, and this, too, can be enhanced by training, monitoring, and continuous education.

Validity

Validity refers to the degree to which a measure assesses what it purports to assess. For example, a test that asks students to recall information would be considered an invalid measure of their ability to apply information. Similarly, an attitude survey will not be considered valid unless it can be proven that people who are identified as satisfied on the basis of their responses to the survey are different in some observable way from people who are identified as dissatisfied.

CONTENT AND FACE VALIDITY

Content validity refers to the extent to which a measure thoroughly and appropriately assesses the skills or characteristics it is intended to assess. For example, an evaluator interested in developing a measure of mental health first has to define the concept (What is mental health? How is health distinguished from disease?) and then write items that adequately include all aspects of the definition. Because of the complexity of the task, the literature often is consulted either for a model or a conceptual framework from which a definition can be derived. It is not uncommon, in establishing content validity, to see a statement like "We used XYZ cognitive theory to select items on mental health, and we adapted the ABC role model paradigm for questions about social relations."

Face validity refers to how a measure appears on the surface: Does it seem to ask all of the needed questions? Does it use the appropriate language and language level to do so? Face validity, unlike content validity, does not rely on established theory for support.

CRITERION VALIDITY

Criterion validity is made up of two subcategories: predictive validity and concurrent validity. **Predictive validity** refers to the extent to which a measure forecasts future performance. A graduate school entry examination that predicts who will do well in graduate school has predictive validity.

Concurrent validity refers to the degree to which two assessments agree or to which a new measure compares favorably with one already considered valid. For example, to establish the concurrent validity of a new aptitude test, the evaluator can administer the new and validated measure to the same group of examinees and compare the scores. Or, the evaluator can administer the new test to the examinees and compare the scores to experts' judgment of students' aptitude. A high correlation between the new test and the criterion measure means concurrent validity. Establishing concurrent validity is useful when a new measure is created whose authors claim is better (shorter, cheaper, fairer).

CONSTRUCT VALIDITY

Construct validity is established experimentally to demonstrate that a measure distinguishes between people who do and do not have certain characteristics. For example, an evaluator who claims construct validity for a measure of competent teaching must prove in a scientific manner that teachers who do well on the measure are more competent than teachers who do poorly.

Construct validity commonly is established in at least two ways. In the first way, the evaluator hypothesizes that the new measure correlates with one or more measures of a similar characteristic (convergent validity) and does not correlate with measures of dissimilar characteristics (discriminant validity). For example, an evaluator validating a new quality-of-life measure might posit that it is highly correlated with another quality-of-life instrument, a measure of functioning, and a measure of health status. At the same time, the evaluator would hypothesize that the new measure does not correlate with selected measures of social desirability (the tendency to answer questions so as to present yourself in a more positive light) and of hostility.

In the second way, the evaluator hypothesizes that the measure can distinguish one group from the other on some important variable. For example, a measure of compassion should demonstrate that high scorers are compassionate but that low scorers are unfeeling. This requires (a) translating a theory of compassionate behavior into measurable terms, (b) identifying compassionate and unfeeling people (according to the theory), and (c) proving that the measure consistently and correctly distinguishes between the two groups.

A Note on Language:
Data Collection Terms

The language that is used to discuss reliability and validity (e.g., **examinees, scores, scales, tests, measures**) comes from test theory or "psychometrics." Program evaluators often use **data source, measure, scale, test,** and **instrument** as synonyms. This use is sometimes confusing, to say the least, especially because evaluators also talk about **outcome measures** or **outcome indicators**. These terms usually refer to an evaluation's outcomes. The following lexicon can be helpful as a guide in sorting out data collection terms.

A Guide to Data Collection Terms

Data source: Any source of information for the evaluation. This may include newly developed measures, such as questionnaires or tests; already-existing data, such as those found in school or case records; and the results of previous evaluations.

Index: A way of rank-ordering things. Scores on an index of satisfaction give an indication of where people stand in relation to one another. Sometimes used interchangeably with **scale**.

Instrument: A synonym for *measure*. A device or strategy used to collect data, including achievement tests, self-administered questionnaires, and interviews.

Measure: Very much like **data source**. Sometimes called **instrument**, **test**, or **assessment**.

Outcome: The consequences of participating in a program, such as acquiring computer skills, the ability to make a documentary, or emotional well-being.

Outcome measure or outcome indicator: Often used as synonyms for **outcome**.

Rating scale: A graded set of choices. These include nominal or categorical scales (e.g., race, gender); ordered or ordinal scales (e.g., often, sometimes, never); numerical scales, including continuous (e.g., age, height) and discrete (e.g., number of absences from school this month, number of books read this year). A most commonly used rating scale is the Likert Scale, with such categories as "strongly agree," "agree," "disagree," and "strongly disagree."

Scale: A combination of items or questions that measure the same concept (e.g., a 10-item scale that measures emotional well-being, a 36-item scale that measures self-confidence).

Test: Usually **test of achievement or knowledge**.

Checklist for Creating a New Measure

Knowing the types of measures that are available and how to demonstrate reliability and validity enables evaluators to get down to the serious business of developing a measure tailored to the needs of their investigation or of selecting and adapting one that is already in use. To create a new measure, an evaluator must have identified the domain of content (through observation or with the help of experts, research, and theory) and have the expertise, time, and money to complete the task. The following sections constitute a checklist of the basic steps in creating a new measure.

_____ **1. Set Boundaries**

____ *Decide on the type of measure* (e.g., questionnaire, observation)

____ *Determine the amount of needed and available time for administration and scoring* (e.g., a 15-minute interview, with 10 minutes for summarizing responses)

____ *Select the kinds of reliability and validity information to collect* (e.g., **alternate-form reliability** means developing two forms; **concurrent validity** means availability of an already-existing instrument)

_____ **2. Define the Subject Matter or Topics**

For definitions, consult the literature, experts, or users. For example, in an evaluation of a program to improve family functioning, the definitions in Example 6.1 were found in the literature and corroborated by psychologists, family counselors, and social workers.

Example 6.1. Defining Terms: Families Are Powerful

Families Are Powerful is a program to improve family functioning. A **family** can refer to the nuclear or traditional family structure or consist of any other arrangement acceptable to the program's participant. A **program** has preset, specific purposes and activities for defined populations and groups. For Families Are Powerful, **family functioning** has three components: satisfaction with family life, overall happiness with family life, and marital functioning.

These definitions tell the evaluator something like the following: If you want to evaluate the Families Are Powerful program, your measures should include attention to satisfaction with family life, overall happiness with family life, and marital functioning. For example, to measure satisfaction with family life, you might ask about satisfaction with the quality of support and understanding, the amount of things talked over, and the amount of cohesion. For overall happiness, you might ask for the degree of happiness (e.g., on a scale ranging from *extremely happy* to *extremely unhappy*). To evaluate marital functioning, you should consider asking questions that describe the degree of intimacy (e.g., being able to say anything you want, sharing personal feelings, ability to rely on one another).

_____ 3. Outline the Content

Suppose that an evaluation was concerned with the outcomes of a family functioning program, such as Families Are Powerful. Assume also that a review of the literature and consultation with experts reveal the importance of collecting data on the following variables: satisfaction with family life and psychological and sexual intimacy with spouse or partner (when appropriate). An outline of the contents might look like this:

Outline of the Contents of a Measure of Outcomes:
Families Are Powerful

I. Satisfaction with family life, especially with

    A. Amount of cohesion

    B. Level of support

    C. Amount of things talked over

II. Overall happiness with family life

III. Intimacy

    A. Sharing feelings

    B. Sexual satisfaction

_____ **4. Select Item-Choices**

The "item" refers to the questions asked of respondents or statements to which they are to react. An example is presented in Box 6.1.

Selecting choices for items requires skill and practice. Whenever possible, use item-choices that others have used effectively. The possibility of finding appropriate choices is greater when collecting demographic information (e.g., age, gender, ethnicity, income, education, where a person lives), for example, than when collecting data

---

Box 6.1. Item-Choices: An Example

Overall, how happy are you with your family life?   Circle one

Choices:

Extremely happy	1
Very happy	2
Somewhat happy	3
Not too happy	4
Somewhat unhappy	5
Extremely unhappy	6

on the knowledge, attitudes, or behaviors that are to result from a specific program designed for a particular group of people. Effective choices can be found in the published and unpublished literature and can be obtained from measures prepared by the U.S. Bureau of the Census; the education and social welfare departments of cities, counties, and states; and other public and private agencies.

_____ **5. Choose Rating Scales**

Rating scales should be adapted from other, proven scales, whenever possible. Like the choices for an item, they can come from measures designed by public and private agencies and those described in the literature. In Box 6.2, a simple true-and-false scale is used.

Box 6.2. Rating Scale: True-False Example

How TRUE or FALSE is each of the following statements.

	1. Definitely True	2. Mostly True	3. Not Sure	4. Mostly False	5. Definitely False
We said anything we wanted to say to each other.	1	2	3	4	5
We often had trouble sharing our personal feelings.	1	2	3	4	5
It was hard to blow off steam with each other.	1	2	3	4	5
We tended to rely on other people for help, rather than on each other.	1	2	3	4	5

_____ **6. Review the Measure With Experts and Potential Users**

Reviews by other evaluators or subject matter experts and potential users are recommended. Questions to ask them are listed below.

Questions to Ask in Reviewing Measures

Ask Experts
    1. Is all relevant content covered?
    2. Is the content covered in adequate depth?
    3. Are all item-choices appropriate?
    4. Are all rating scales appropriate?
    5. Is the measure too long?

Ask Users
    1. Is all relevant content covered?
    2. Is the content covered in adequate depth?
    3. Do you understand without ambiguity all item-choices and scales?
    4. Did you have enough time to complete the measure?
    5. Did you have enough time to administer the measure?
    6. Is the measure too long?

_____ **7. Revise the Measure**

Revise the measure on the basis of comments.

_____ **8. Add a Coding Strip**

A code has two components: a number for the response (e.g., yes = 1 and no = 2) and information for the data enterer regarding in which "column" or space to put a respondent's reply. The coding strip may be placed directly on the measure as long as it does not clutter the format of the measure. Typical strips are shown in Example 6.2.

Example 6.2. Example of Coding Strips

A. During the past 7 days, how many times did you eat broccoli? (Circle ONE choice)

Once	1	*20*
Two or three times	2	
Four or more	3	
I did not eat any broccoli	4	

B. In the last week, did you eat any of the following? (Circle one for each choice of food)

	CIRCLE ONE		
	1. Yes	2. No	
Broccoli	1	2	*20*
Hamburger	1	2	*21*
Chicken	1	2	*22*
Spinach	1	2	*23*
Potatoes	1	2	*24*

Or

C. Which of these did you eat in the last week? (Check all that apply)

[ ] Broccoli	*20*
[ ] Hamburger	*21*
[ ] Chicken	*22*
[ ] Spinach	*23*
[ ] Potatoes	*24*
[ ] I ate none of these.	*25*

The numbers to the right of the item are the "columns" or places for recording the responses to each item. To the data enterer, it works this way:

What the Data Enterer Does for Items A, B, and C

Item A: In column 20, place 1, 2, 3, or 4 (depending on the person's response).

Item B: In columns 20, 21, 22, 23, and 24, place 1 or 2 (depending on the person's response).

Item C: In columns 20, 21, 22, 23, 24, and 25, place 1 if checked; place 2 if not checked.

If an item is left blank, the column must be assigned some number, such as 9 (assuming 8 or fewer choices). If nine choices or more, can you use another code—say, 99? Yes, but then you must provide for data entry into two columns, and the numbers would be entered as 01, 02, . . . 99. Example 6.3 illustrates coding strips for items with more than nine choices or a double-digit answer.

Example 6.3. Coding Strips for Items With More Than Nine Choices or With a Double-Digit Answer

D. What was your total household income before taxes in 1994?

[ ]	$10,000 or less	*20-21*
[ ]	$10,001 to $12,000	
[ ]	$12,001 to $15,000	
[ ]	$15,001 to $20,000	
[ ]	$20,001 to $30,000	
[ ]	$30,001 to $40,000	
[ ]	$40,001 to $50,000	
[ ]	$50,001 to $70,000	
[ ]	$70,001 to $90,000	
[ ]	Over $90,000	

E. How many people in your household are supported by your total household income?

Write in number of household members:

___   ___   *50-51*

A **skip pattern** refers to one or more items that a respondent does not have to complete because the items are not pertinent (see Example 6.4).

Example 6.4. Coding Strip for an Item With a Skip Pattern

Have you ever been told to stop chewing gum by a teacher or other school official?

1	[ ] NO →	**Go to question 8**	*21*
2	[ ] YES →	Did you stop	
		chewing the gum?	
		1 [ ] yes	*22*
		2 [ ] no	

As a rule, skip patterns should be used only with skilled observers and interviewers. Avoid skip patterns in self-administered surveys.

_____ **9. Put the Measure in an Appropriate Format**

The following list gives an example of an appropriate format:

_____ Add an ID code; without it, you cannot match data collected on the same person over time.

_____ Add directions for administration and completion.

_____ Add a statement regarding confidentiality (persons are identifiable by code) or anonymity (no means of identification).

_____ Add thank-you's.

_____ Give instructions for submitting the completed measure. If mailed, is an addressed and stamped envelope provided? By what date should the measure be completed?

_____ **10. Review and Test Measure Before Administration**

The importance of pilot testing a new measure cannot be overemphasized. A **pilot test** is use of the measure in realistic conditions. This means using the measure with as many participants as the evaluation's resources will allow. After they have completed the measure, interview the participants to determine any problems they might have had. With interviews, the methods for interviewing, as well for answering the questions, should be tested.

Checklist for Selecting
an Already-Existing Measure

Many instruments and measures are available for use by program evaluators. A good source for them is the published evaluations found in journals. In some cases, the whole instrument is published as part of the article. If not, the "methods" section usually describes all main data sources and measures, and the evaluator can contact the authors for additional information.

Using an already-tested measure has many advantages. Among them is the hope of saving time and other resources needed to develop and validate a completely new instrument. Choosing a measure that has been used elsewhere, however, is not without pitfalls. You may be required to pay for the measure, share your data, or substantially modify the measure, thus jeopardizing its reliability and validity and requiring you to establish them all over again.

The following sections constitute a checklist for choosing an already-existing measure.

_____ **1. Find Out the Costs**

Do you have to pay? share data? share authorship?

_____ **2. Check the Content**

In essence, you must do your own face and content validity study. Make sure the questions are the ones you would ask if you were developing the instrument. Check the choices and rating scales. Will they get you the information you need?

_____ **3. Check the Reliability and Validity**

Are the types of reliability and validity that have been confirmed appropriate for your needs? If you are interested in interrater reliability but only internal consistency statistics are provided, the measure may not be the right one. If you are interested in a measure's ability to predict but only content validity data are available, think again before adopting the instrument.

Check carefully the context in which the measure has been validated. Are the settings and groups similar to those in your evaluation? If not, the instrument may not be valid for your purposes. For example, a measure of compliance with counselors' advice in a program to prevent child abuse and neglect that has been tested on teen mothers in Helena, Montana, may not be applicable to nonteen mothers in Helena, Montana, or to teen mothers in San Francisco, California.

The evaluator also must decide whether a measure is sufficiently reliable and valid for use. Reliability and validity often are described as correlations (say, between experts or measures or among items). How high should the correlations be? The fast answer is the higher, the better, and that .90 is best, but the statistic by itself should not be the only or even the most important criterion. A lower correlation may be acceptable if the measure has other properties that are potentially more important. For example, the content may be especially appropriate or the measure might have been tested on participants that are very much like those in the present evaluation.

_____ **4. Check the Measure's Format**

♦ Will the data collectors be able to score the measure?

♦ Does it make sense to use it, given your available technology? For example, if it requires certain software or expertise, do you have it? Can you afford to get it?

♦ Will the participants in the evaluation be willing to complete the measure? Participants sometimes object to spending more than 10 or 15 minutes on an interview, for example. Also, personal questions and complicated instructions can result in incomplete data.

The Measurement Chart: Logical Connections

A measurement chart assists the evaluator in the logistics of the evaluation by ensuring that all variables will have the appropriate coverage. The chart is also useful in writing proposals because it portrays the logical connections among what is being measured, how, for how long, and with whom. When writing reports, the chart provides a summary of some of the important features of the evaluation's data sources. Look at the measurement chart in Table 6.1. Each column of the chart attempts to make logical connections among the segments of data collection.

Dependent Variables. The measurement chart tells about the dependent variables, or the aspects of knowledge, skill, attitude, and behavior the program aims to modify. Suppose a preventive health education program for high school students (the Health Assessment and Prevention Program for Youth—HAPPY) has as its purpose to favorably change knowledge, beliefs, self-confidence, and behav-

Table 6.1. Measurement Chart

Dependent Variables	How Measured	Sample	Timing and Administration	Duration of Measurements	Content	Reliability and Validity	General Concerns
Knowledge	20-item achievement test; score is the percentage correct	All 739 students in 29 experimental and 577 students in 23 control classes	Approximately 2 weeks before and 3 months after curriculum implementation; trained teachers will administer and collect the test	About 30 minutes	Knowledge of preventive health practices, including good nutrition, adequate exercise and sleep, and safe sexual practices	The 20 items are rated as essential by the U.S. Center for Well-Being and have been extensively tried out and used with thousands of high school students (content validity). A 10% sample (120 students) will be tested 2 weeks after baseline to ascertain reliability (test-retest).	No costs will be incurred, as the center is a government agency. Because the measurements composed a customary evaluation of a school instructional program, parental consent was waived by the board of education. No special software or hardware is necessary.

continued

159

Table 6.1. (Continued)

Dependent Variables	How Measured	Sample	Timing and Administration	Duration of Measurements	Content	Reliability and Validity	General Concerns
Beliefs	Self-administered questionnaire survey: 25 items. Items in each scale are assigned numerical values and added to get scores.	All 739 students in 29 experimental and 577 students in 23 control classes	Approximately 2 weeks before and 3 months after curriculum implementation; trained teachers administer and collect the survey	About 45 minutes	Five items on perceived susceptibility to getting sick and 10 items respectively asking about perceived physical and psychological benefits of and barriers to health preventive activities by teens	The items were created for the evaluation and based on aspects of the health behavior model (content validity).	
Self-confidence	Interviews: 22 items; items are assigned numerical values and added to get scores	A random sample of 200 students in 29 experimental and 100 students in 23 control classes	Within 3 months of the program's completion, trained evaluation staff will conduct the interviews.	About 30 minutes to interview; 10 minutes for interviewer to review each and ensure readiness for data entry	Confidence in ability to make decisions about health (when to obtain health care, dietary patterns, amount of exercise, use of abusive substances)	Items based on cognitive theory (content validity)	

Table 6.1. (Continued)

Dependent Variables	How Measured	Sample	Timing and Administration	Duration of Measurements	Content	Reliability and Validity	General Concerns
Behaviors	Self-administered questionnaire: 30 items; items are assigned numerical values and added to get scores	739 students in 29 experimental and 577 students in 23 control classes	Approximately 2 weeks before and 3 months after curriculum implementation; trained teachers administer and collect the survey	About 30 minutes	Types of food eaten for lunch within the past 2 weeks, types of exercise, symptoms, sleep patterns, sexual patterns	All items taken from Health Inventory Program (HIP). Validated on teens throughout the U.S. Shown to predict use of health services and to discriminate between youths who continue to practice prevention and those who do not [cite source]	

iors. These are the dependent variables, and they are listed in the first column of the chart.

Measures. For each variable, the type of measure should be indicated. The measurement chart shows that knowledge will be assessed with a 20-item achievement test; beliefs and behaviors with 25- and 30-item questionnaires, respectively; and self-confidence with a 22-item interview. The method of assigning scores also is given. For the knowledge test, the score is the percentage of correctly answered questions. For the other measures, the score is a numerical value.

Sample. A **sample** is the number and characteristics of individuals who will constitute the sample for each measure. The measurement chart shows that the entire population of students will be assessed to find out about knowledge, beliefs, and behavior. To find out about self-confidence, a sample of 300 (200 in the experimental and 100 in the control) will be interviewed.

Timing and Administration. The **timing** refers to when each measure is to be administered. For example, the chart shows that to measure knowledge, behaviors, and beliefs, students will be assessed twice: approximately 2 weeks before and 3 months after curriculum implementation. To measure self-confidence, students will be interviewed only once, within 3 months of the program's completion. This section of the measurement chart also tells who will administer the measure. Classroom teachers will be trained to administer all of the tests and surveys. The evaluation team will conduct the interviews.

Duration of Measurements. The amount of time each measure will take to administer and summarize or score is the **duration**. All students will have 105 minutes of tests and surveys at two points in time: about 2 weeks before and 3 months after curriculum implementation. The sample of students to be interviewed will have another 30 minutes. The interviewers will need an additional 10 minutes to check over each completed interview and prepare it for data entry.

Content. A brief description of the content is provided in the chart. For example, **knowledge** includes preventive health practices, such as good nutrition, adequate exercise and sleep, and safe sexual practices.

Reliability and Validity. The measurement chart describes the planned types of reliability and validity. For example, the knowledge test will be taken from one that experts agree comprises essential learning (content validity) and that is likely to be reliable and valid for teens because it has been used extensively with high school students. Nevertheless, the evaluators plan to compute test-retest reliability statistics. Measures of self-confidence and belief are new and based on theory; the assumption is that they have content validity. The behaviors measures, however, have construct validity because they are based on research that shows performance can be used to predict use of health services and to distinguish between teens who continue to practice prevention and those who do not.

General Concerns. In this portion of the chart, any special features of the entire data collection and measurement endeavor should be noted. These include costs, training, number of items, special software or hardware requirements, and issues pertaining to informed consent.

SUMMARY AND TRANSITION TO NEXT CHAPTER ON DATA ANALYSIS

Having reliable and valid measures is essential in a diligent evaluation. Sometimes, the evaluator is required or chooses to create a new measure; at other times, a measure is available that appears to be suitable. Whether creating, adapting, or adopting, the evaluator must critically review the measure to ensure its appropriateness and accuracy for the present study.

A measurement chart is a useful way of showing the relationships among dependent variables, how and when and by whom the dependent variables are measured, and the content, reliability, and validity of the measures. A measurement chart can be used in planning and reporting on evaluations.

The next chapter on analysis discusses the most commonly used methods of data analysis in program evaluations. To choose among them requires identifying the independent and dependent variables and understanding the nature of the evaluation's data and the measurement scales from which they are derived. The chapter also provides information on how to assess statistical and educational significance and how to use meta-analysis to combine the results of relatively small, local studies. Practical concerns, such as cleaning and transforming data and preparing a codebook with instructions for data entry, also are addressed.

EXERCISES: EVALUATION MEASURES

EXERCISE 1. RELIABILITY AND VALIDITY

Directions

Read the following scenarios and tell which subconcepts of reliability and validity are covered.

A. The self-administered questionnaire was adapted with minor revisions from the Student Health Risk Questionnaire, which is designed to investigate knowledge, attitudes, behaviors, and various other cognitive variables regarding HIV and AIDS among high school students. Four behavior scales measured sexual activity (4 questions in each scale) and needle use (5 questions); 23 items determined a scale of factual knowledge regarding AIDS. Cognitive variables derived from the health belief model and social learning theory were employed to examine personal beliefs and social norms (12 questions).

B. More than 150 counseling records were reviewed by a single reviewer; a subset of 35 records was reviewed by a second blinded expert to assess the validity of the review. Rates of agreement for single items ranged from 81% ($\kappa = .77$, $p < .001$) to 100% ($\kappa = 1$, $p < .001$).

C. Group A and Group B supervisors of curriculum and instruction were given a 22-question quiz testing evaluation principles derived from UCLA guidelines. It was not scored in a blinded manner, but each test was scored twice.

EXERCISE 2. CREATING AND CODING MEASURES

Directions

Imagine you are the evaluator of an experimental program to counsel students having social and behavioral problems at school. The program involves students and their families in individual and group sessions. Special family and student support groups are available. As part of the evaluation, you develop a self-administered questionnaire for counselors, asking them to describe the effects of the program on each participating student. For example, one question (see Box 6.3) asks whether the student has improved in his or her ability to cope.

Box 6.3

Rate the extent of improvement in this student's ability to cope with school.

(Circle **one** choice only)

Much improvement	1	*34*
Some improvement	2	
Marginal improvement	3	
Little or no improvement	4	
Insufficient opportunity to observe	9	

Other questions ask about the student's ability to get to school on time, manage time appropriately, and maintain satisfactory relationships with other students and teachers. (a) Create a form for obtaining this information and (b) add a coding strip.

EXERCISE 3. REVIEWING A DATA COLLECTION PLAN

Directions

Read the following information collection plan and, acting as an independent reviewer, provide the evaluator with a description of your problems and concerns.

The School of Education is in the process of revising its elective course in educational evaluation. As part of the process, a survey to determine whether and to what extent topics in research design and sampling are taught was sent to all faculty who currently teach evaluation. Among the school's objectives is to improve students' knowledge of research design and sampling and their attitudes toward the importance of acquiring a sound background in these topics. The results of the faculty survey revealed little coverage of either design or sampling. Many faculty indicated that they would teach more but that they were lacking practical educational materials and did not have the resources to prepare their own. To rectify this deficiency, a course with materials was developed and disseminated. The Center for Education and Evaluation was asked to appraise the effectiveness of the educational materials.

Evaluators from the center prepared a series of knowledge and skills tests and planned to administer them to students each year over a 5-year period. The Center for Education and Evaluation has a team of experts in test construction, so the evaluators decided to omit pilot testing and save the time and expense. Their purpose in testing was to measure changes (if any) in students' knowledge and skills. They also planned to interview a sample of cooperating students to get in-depth portraits of the strengths and weaknesses of the materials.

Suggested Readings

American Psychological Association (APA). (1985). *Standards for educational and psychological testing.* Washington, DC: Author.

A classic work on reliability and validity and the standards that testers should achieve to ensure accuracy.

Babbie, E. B. (1992). *The practice of social research.* Belmont, CA: Wadsworth.

A textbook that contains useful discussions on various evaluation topics, including measurement. Criteria for measuring reliability and validity are discussed, as well as how to design scales and indexes.

Bandura, A. (1986). *Social foundations of thought and action: A social cognitive theory.* Englewood Cliffs, NJ: Prentice Hall.

Bandura is one of the leading exponents of social cognitive theory, and this book is well worth reading for those interested in the field.

Becker, M. (1974). The health belief model and personal health behavior. *Health Education Monographs, 2,* 326-373.

The health belief model discussed in this monograph and other works by Becker is used by health educators to explain susceptibility to illness from a value-expectancy theoretical framework. In general, the model assumes that feeling susceptible is based on a person's current and prior experiences with health problems.

Hambleton, R. K., & Zaal, J. N. (Eds.). (1991). *Advances in educational and psychological testing.* Boston: Kluwer Academic.

Important source of information on the concepts of *reliability* and *validity* in education and psychological testing.

Morris, L. L., Fitz-Gibbon, C. T., & Lindheim, E. (1987). *How to measure performance and use tests* (*Program evaluation kit,* 2nd ed., series edited by J. L. Herman). Newbury Park, CA: Sage.

Excellent discussion and illustration of reliability and validity in measuring students' performance as an indicator of program effectiveness.

Sudman, S., & Bradburn, N. M. (1982). *Asking questions.* San Francisco: Jossey-Bass.

Poor questions lead to inaccurate data. This book is an important source of information on how to ask questions correctly to get reliable and valid results.

Purpose of This Chapter

Program evaluators use statistical methods to analyze and summarize data and to come to conclusions that can be applied to program planning and policy. Choosing a method to analyze program evaluation data is an intellectual process in which statistical technology and the outcomes of interventions and programs converge. This chapter discusses key components of the intellectual process.

In specific, this chapter addresses the associations among the evaluation questions, design, sample, and data sources and shows how the choice of analysis is as much a function of the characteristics of the evaluation question and the quality of the data available to evaluators as it is dependent on their ability to identify the appropriate statistical technique. The chapter does not focus on how to perform statistical operations (better covered in statistics texts and computer manuals) but does focus on the pertinent uses of the procedures most commonly employed by program evaluators. Practice in reading and interpreting computer output also is provided.

Analyzing Evaluation Data

A Suitable Analysis:
Starting With the Evaluation Questions

To select the most suitable analysis for evaluation, the evaluator must answer these four questions:

1. What independent and dependent variables are contained within each evaluation question (and its associated standard)?
2. In what form or from what kind of scale will data be provided? Data can come from nominal scales (e.g., male, female); ordinal scales (e.g., high, medium, low); and numerical scales (e.g., a score of 30 out of 100 possible points).
3. What statistical methods may be used to answer the evaluation question, given its independent and dependent variables?
4. Do the evaluation's data meet all assumptions of the statistical tests? (e.g., Is the sample size sufficient? Are the data "normally distributed"?)

Measurement Scales and Their Data

A first step in selecting a statistical method is to identify the types of data resulting from each measure used to collect data on the independent and dependent variables. A **variable** is a characteristic that is measurable. Mass is a variable, and all persons having a mass of 55 kg have the same numerical mass. Satisfaction is also a variable. In this case, however, the numerical scale must be devised and rules created for its interpretation. For example, in Evaluation A, teacher satisfaction may be measured on a scale of 1 to 100, with 1 corresponding to the very lowest satisfaction and 100 to the very highest. In Evaluation B, teacher satisfaction may be measured by counting the proportion of teachers who stay in the district for 5 or more years, and if the number equals a preset standard, then participants will be considered satisfied.

Independent variables are used to explain or predict a program's outcomes (or dependent variables). Typical independent variables in program evaluations include group membership (experimental and control), age, and other demographic characteristics. Dependent variables are outcomes, such as skills, attitudes, knowledge, and efficiency and quality of teaching and learning.

Evaluators most often rely on three types of measurement scales: nominal, ordinal, and numerical. In turn, the data they produce are called "nominal," "ordinal," and "numerical" data or variables or observations.

NOMINAL SCALES

Nominal scales produce data that fit into categories. Thus, they sometimes are called "categorical." Two are shown below.

1. What is your gender?	(Circle one)
Male	1
Female	2
2. Name the statistical method.	**(Circle one)**
Chi-square	1
ANOVA	2
Independent samples *t* test	3
Regression	4

Both questions categorize the responses and require the answer to "name" the category into which the data fit.

Typically, nominal data are described as percentages and proportions (e.g., 50 of 100 [50%] of the sample was male). The measure used to describe the center of their distribution is the **mode**, or the category of observations that appears most frequently.

ORDINAL SCALES

If an inherent order exists among categories, the data are said to be obtained from an ordinal scale. Two are shown below.

How much education have you completed?   (Circle one)

Never finished high school   1
High school graduate, but no college   2
Some college   3
College graduate   4

Indicate the extent of agreement   (Circle
or disagreement.   one)

Strongly agree   1
Agree   2
Disagree   3
Strongly disagree   4

Variables whose characteristics can be arranged or ordered by class (e.g., high, medium, and low); quality (e.g., highly positive, positive, negative, strongly negative); and degree (e.g., very conservative, somewhat conservative, somewhat liberal, very liberal). Ordinal scales are used to ask questions that call for ratings of how the respondent feels (e.g., excellent, very good, good, fair, poor, very poor), whether the respondent agrees (e.g., strongly agree, agree, disagree, strongly disagree), and the respondent's opinion regarding the probability that something is present (e.g., definitely present, probably present, probably not present, definitely not present).

Percentages and proportions are used with ordinal data, and the center of the distribution often is expressed as the **median,** or the observation that divides the distribution into two halves. The median is equal to the 50th percentile.

NUMERICAL (INTERVAL AND RATIO) SCALES

When differences between numbers have a meaning on a numerical scale, they are **numerical.** For example, age is a numerical variable, and so are weight and length of survival with a disease.

Numerical data are amenable to precision, so the evaluator can obtain data on age to the nearest second, for example.

Some evaluators and educational researchers distinguish between interval and ratio scales. **Ratio scales** have a true 0-point (as in the absolute zero value of the Kelvin temperature scale). In program evaluations, however, ratio scales are extremely rare, and statistically, interval and ratio scales are treated the same. The term **numerical** is a more apt (and neutral) word.

Numerical data can be continuous (e.g., height, weight, age) or discrete (e.g., number of days absent, number of books read). Means and standard deviations (discussed later) are used to summarize the values of numerical measures.

Figure 7.1 contrasts the types of scales and data that are essential in choosing methods of analysis.

Selecting a Method of Analysis

The choice of method to use in analyzing data for each evaluation question is dependent on the following:

- whether the independent variable is nominal, ordinal, or numerical
- the number of independent variables
- whether the dependent variable is nominal, ordinal, or numerical
- the number of dependent variables
- whether the design, sampling, and quality of the data meet the assumptions of the statistical method

The list on page 175 shows the relationships among evaluation questions, independent and dependent variables, research design and sample, types of measures, and data analysis.

Measurement Scale and Type of Data	Examples	Comments
Nominal	Ethnicity; gender; political party affiliation; place of birth, location of school; hair color	Observations belong to categories. Observations have no inherent order of importance. Observations sometimes are called "nominal" or "categorical." When data assume two values (yes, students read at grade level; no, they do not), they are termed "dichotomous." Percentages and proportions are used to describe nominal data; the mode is used to measure the midpoint.
Ordinal	Socioeconomic status; degree (extent of agreement); class (higher, lower); and quality (good, fair, poor)	Order exists among the categories; that is, one observation is greater than the other. Percentages and proportions are used to describe ordinal data; the measure of the center of the distribution of the data is often the median.
Numerical	Continuous numerical scales: scores on a test of intelligence; age; height; length of survival Discrete numerical scales: number of visits to the school nurse; number of books read	Differences between numbers have meaning on a numerical scale (e.g., higher scores mean better achievement than lower scores, and a difference between 12 and 13 has the same meaning as a difference between 99 and 100). Some evaluators distinguish between interval scales (arbitrary 0-point, as in the Fahrenheit temperature scale) and ratio scales (with an absolute 0, as in the Kelvin temperature scale); in program evaluation, these measures are treated the same statistically, so they are combined here as numerical. Means and standard deviations are used to describe numerical data.

Figure 7.1. Measurement Scales: Nominal, Ordinal, and Numerical Variables

Analyzing Evaluation Data:
Illustrative Connections Among Questions, Designs, Samples, Measures, and Analysis

Evaluation question: Is the quality of day care satisfactory?

Standard: A statistically significant difference in quality of day care favoring program versus control program participants

Independent variable: Group membership (participants vs. controls)

Design: An experimental design with concurrent controls

Sampling: Eligible participants are assigned at random to experimental and control groups. Each group contains 150 participants (a statistically derived sample size).

Dependent variable: Quality of day care

Types of data: Group membership (nominal data); quality of day care (numerical data: data are from the DAYCARES Questionnaire, a 100-point survey in which higher scores mean better quality)

Analysis: A two-sample independent group *t* test

Justification for the analysis: This *t* test is appropriate when the independent variable is measured on a nominal scale and the dependent variable is measured on a numerical scale. In this case, the assumptions of a *t* test are met: (a) Each group has a sample size of at least 30, (b) the sizes of the groups are about equal, (c) the two groups are independent (an assumption that is met most easily with a strong evaluation design and a high-quality data collection effort), and (d) the data are normally distributed. (If one of the assumptions is seriously violated, other rigorous analytic methods should be used, such as the Wilcoxon Rank-Sum Test, also called the Mann-Whitney *U* test. This test makes no assumption about the normality of the distribution; whereas the *t* test is *parametric,* this test is one of a number *nonparametric.* For more information, see the appropriate suggested readings at the end of the chapter.)

The classification of data into nominal, ordinal, and numerical is a guide for the program evaluator. Each evaluation and set of data will vary. For the sake of simplicity, for example, sometimes independent variables measured on an ordinal scale are treated as if they were nominal. Also, dependent variables measured on an ordinal scale are treated as if they were numerical. Other exceptions exist as well. Example 7.1 shows some of some of these exceptions.

Example 7.1. Some Exceptions: Taking Liberties With Nominal, Ordinal, and Numerical Data

Evaluation question: How do parents with differing educational levels compare in their satisfaction with federally funded preschools?

Independent variable: Educational level

Measurement scale: Ordinal: college graduate; some college; high school graduate; has not completed high school; in choosing an analytic method, treat educational level as nominal

Dependent variable: Satisfaction (with federally funded preschools)

Measurement scale: Numerical: Scores on the Parent Satisfaction Survey

Analysis: One-way ANOVA (presuming the necessary assumptions are met)

Evaluation question: How do people of differing ages compare in their satisfaction with their local schools?

Independent variable: Age

Measurement scale: Numerical (ratio); in choosing an analytic method, treat as nominal with only two values: under 55 years and over 55 years

Dependent variable: Numerical: Scores on Parent Satisfaction Survey

Analysis: t test (presuming the necessary assumptions are met)

Unfortunately, no definitive rules can be set for all evaluations and their data. However, Figure 7.2 is a general guide to the selection of 15 of the most commonly used data-analytic methods. (Statistical calculations are not covered in this book. For statistics texts, see the suggested readings at the end of the chapter.)

Sample Questions	Type of Data: Independent Variable	Type of Data: Dependent Variable	Potential Analytic Method*
For questions with one independent and one dependent variable:			
Do participants in the experimental and control groups differ in their use or failure to use mental health services?	Nominal: group (experimental and control)	Nominal: use of mental health services (used services or did not)	Chi-square; Fisher's exact test; relative risk (risk ratio); odds ratio
How do the experimental and control groups compare in their attitudes (measured by their scores on the attitude survey)?	Nominal (dichotomous): group (experimental and control)	Numerical: attitude scores	Independent samples *t* test
How do teens in the U.S., Canada, and England compare in their attitudes (measured by their scores on the attitude survey)?	Nominal (more than two values: U.S., Canada, and England)	Numerical: attitude scores	one-way ANOVA (uses the *F* test)
Do high scores on the attitude survey predict high scores on the knowledge test?	Numerical (attitude scores)	Numerical (knowledge scores)	Regression (when neither variable is independent or dependent, use correlation)

continued

Figure 7.2. A General Guide to Data-Analytic Methods in Program Evaluation

NOTE: *For more information on each analytic method, see the appropriate suggested reading at the end of the chapter.

Sample Questions	Type of Data: Independent Variable	Type of Data: Dependent Variable	Potential Analytic Method[*]
For questions with two or more independent variables:			
Do men and women in the experimental and control programs differ in whether or not they attended at least one parent-teacher conference?	Nominal (gender, group)	Nominal (attended or did not attend at least one parent-teacher conference)	Log-linear
Do men and women with differing scores on the knowledge test differ in whether or not they attended at least one parent-teacher conference?	Nominal (gender) and numerical (knowledge scores)	Nominal and dichotomous (attended or did not attend at least one parent-teacher conference)	Logistic regression
How do men and women in the experimental and control programs compare in their attitudes (measured by their scores on the attitude survey)?	Nominal (gender and group)	Numerical (attitude scores)	Analysis of variance (ANOVA)
How are age and income and years living in the community related to attitudes (measured by scores on the attitude survey)?	Numerical (age and income and years living in the community)	Numerical (attitude scores)	Multiple regression
How do men and women in the experimental and control programs compare in their attitudes (measured by their scores on the attitude survey) when their level of education is controlled?	Nominal (gender and group) with confounding factors (e.g., education)	Numerical (attitude score)	Analysis of covariance (ANCOVA)

continued

Figure 7.2. (Continued)

Sample Questions	Type of Data: Independent Variable	Type of Data: Dependent Variable	Potential Analytic Method[*]
For questions with two or more independent and dependent variables:			
How do men and women in the experimental and control programs compare in their attitude and knowledge scores?	Nominal (gender and group)	Numerical (scores on two measures: attitudes and knowledge)	Multivariate analysis of variance (MANOVA)

Figure 7.2. (Continued)

To use the guide, the evaluator must identify the number and measurement characteristics of the independent and dependent variables.

For simplicity, the guide omits ordinal variables. When independent variables are measured on an ordinal scale, they often are treated as if they were nominal. For example, an evaluation whose aim is to predict the outcomes of participation in a program with good, fair, and poor functional status can regard good, fair, and poor (ordinal, independent variables) as nominal. When dependent variables are measured on an ordinal scale, they habitually are treated as if they were numerical. For example, if the dependent variable in a counseling program is the amount of time spent on homework each day (less than 15 minutes, between 15 and 60 minutes, and more than 60 minutes) by boys and girls with differing motivations, the dependent, ordinal variable can, for the sake of the analysis, be regarded as numerical.

Remember to check the assumptions (in a statistics text or computer manual) before conducting any statistical analysis. If the evaluation's data do not meet the assumptions, look for other statistical methods to use. Statistical methods are continuously advancing, and new methods may be emerging that meet the needs of a particular program evaluation.

Hypothesis Testing, *p* Values, and Confidence Intervals: Statistical and Practical Significance

Evaluators often compare two or more groups to determine whether differences in outcomes exist that favor a program; if differences are present, the magnitude of those differences are examined for significance. Consider Example 7.2.

Example 7.2.

Evaluation question: Do students improve in their knowledge of how to interpret food label information when choosing snacks?

Standards:

1. A statistically significant difference in knowledge between participating and nonparticipating students must be found. The difference in scores must be at least 15 points.

2. If a 15-point difference is found, participants will be studied for 2 years to determine the extent to which the knowledge is retained. The scores must be maintained (no significant differences) over the 2-year period.

Measurements: Knowledge is measured on a 25-item test.

Analysis: A *t* test will be used to compare the two groups of students in their knowledge. Scores will be computed a second time, and a *t* test will be used to compare the average or mean differences over time.

In this example, tests of statistical significance are called for twice: to compare participating and nonparticipating students at one point in time, and to compare the same participants' scores over time. In addition, the stipulation is that for the scores to have practical or educational meaning, a 15-point difference between participants and nonparticipants must be obtained and sustained. With experience, program evaluators have found that, in a number of situations, statistical significance is sometimes insufficient evidence of a program's merit. With very large samples, for example, very small differences in numerical values (e.g., scores on an achievement test) can be statistically significant but have little practical or educational meaning and actually may incur more costs than benefits.

In Example 7.2, the standard includes a 15-point difference in test scores. If the difference between scores is statistically significant by only 10 points, then the program will not be considered educationally significant.

STATISTICAL SIGNIFICANCE AND THE *p* VALUE

A statistically significant program evaluation effect is one that probably is due to a planned intervention, rather than to some chance occurrence. To determine statistical significance, the evaluator restates the evaluation question as a null hypothesis and sets the level of significance and the value the test statistic must obtain to be significant. After this is completed, the calculations are performed. The guidelines on pp. 182-184 are for conducting a hypothesis test and for determining statistical significance.

PRACTICAL SIGNIFICANCE:
USING CONFIDENCE INTERVALS

The results of a statistical analysis may be significant, but not necessarily practical or educationally meaningful.

Evaluation 1. Suppose, in a national evaluation of an elementary school science program, 480 students of 800 (60%) respond well to the new program, while 416 of the 800 (52%) do well in the traditional or standard program. Through a chi-square to assess the existence of a real difference between the two programs, a *p* value of .001 is obtained (see Figure 7.4). This value is the probability of

A Guide to Hypothesis Testing,
Statistical Significance, and p Values

1. *State the evaluation question as a null hypothesis.* The null hypothesis (H_0) is a statement that no difference exists between the averages or means of two groups. For example, following are typical null hypotheses in program evaluations:

♦ No difference exists between the experimental and the control programs' means.

♦ No difference exists between the sample's (the evaluation's participants) mean and the population's mean (the population from which the participants were sampled).

When evaluators find that a difference does not exist between means, the terminology used is, "We failed to reject the null hypothesis." Do not say, "We accepted the null hypothesis." Failing to reject the null suggests that a difference probably does *not* exist between the means—for example, between the mean opinion scores in School A versus School B. If the null is rejected, then a difference probably exists between the mean opinion scores. Until the data are examined, however, the evaluator does not know whether School A or School B is favored. When the evaluator has no advance knowledge of which is favored, a two-tailed hypothesis test is used. When the evaluator has an alternative hypothesis in mind—for example, A is favored over B—a one-tailed test is used.

2. *State the level of significance for the statistical test (e.g., the t test) being used.* The level of significance, when chosen before the test is performed, is called the "alpha value" (denoted by the Greek letter alpha: α). The alpha gives the probability of rejecting the null hypothesis when it is actually true. Tradition keeps the alpha value small—.05, .01, or .001—because among the last things an evaluator wants is to reject a null hypothesis when, in fact, it is true and there is no difference between group means.

Guidelines *(Continued)*

The p value is the probability that an observed result (or result of a statistical test) is due to chance (and not to the program). It is calculated *after* the statistical test. If the p value is less than alpha, then the null hypothesis is rejected.

Current practice requires the specification of exact p values; that is, if the obtained p is .03, report that number, rather than $p < .05$. Reporting the approximate p was common practice before the widespread use of computers (when statistical tables were the primary source of probabilities). The practice has not been eradicated, however. The merits of using the exact values can be seen in that, without them, a finding of $p = .06$ may be viewed as not significant, while a finding of $p = .05$ will be.

3. *Determine the value that the test statistic must attain to be significant.* The values can be found in statistical tables. For example, for the z distribution (a standard, normal distribution) with an alpha of .05, and a two-tailed test, tabular values (found in practically all statistics books) will show that the area of acceptance for the null hypothesis is the central 95% of the z distribution and that the areas of rejection are the 2.5% of the area in each tail. The value of z (found in statistical tables) that defines these areas is -1.96 for the lower tail and $+1.96$ for the upper tail. If the test statistic is less than -1.96 or greater than $+1.96$, it will be rejected. The areas of acceptance and rejection in a standard normal distribution using $\alpha = .05$ are illustrated in Figure 7.3.

4. *Perform the calculation.* Numerous statistical packages are available for making statistical computations. Each of the packages has a manual and/or tutorial that teaches how to enter data and perform the calculations. To understand the assumptions that underlie each test and the basis for the calculations, consult a statistics text or, when available, the special manuals and programs that accompany statistical packages.

Guidelines (Continued)

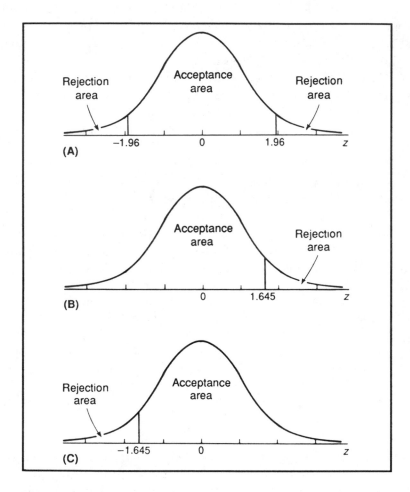

Figure 7.3. Areas of Acceptance and Rejection in a Standard Normal Distribution, Using $\alpha = 0.5$

NOTE: Defining areas of acceptance and rejection in standard normal distribution, using $\alpha = 0.5$; (A) two-tailed or nondirectional; (B) one-tailed or directional upper tail; (C) one-tailed or directional lower tail.
SOURCE: Dawson-Saunders and Trapp (1994). *Basic and clinical biostatistics* (2nd ed., Norwalk, CT: Appleton & Lange), p. 74; used by permission.

obtaining by chance the 8-point (60% to 52%) difference between students in the new and traditional programs or an even larger difference. The point estimate is 8 percentage points, but because of sampling and measurement errors (they always exist in evaluation research), the estimate is probably not identical to the true percentage difference between the two groups of students. A **confidence interval** (CI) provides a plausible range for the true value. A confidence interval is computed from sample data; the interval has a given probability that the unknown true value is located between them. With a standard method, the 95% confidence interval (95% CI) of the 8-percentage-point-difference comes out to be between 3% and 13%. A 95% CI means that about 95% of all such intervals would include the unknown true difference and 5% would not. Suppose, however, that, given the side effects and other costs of the new program, the smallest educational and thus acceptable difference (determined during the standard-setting step of the evaluation process) is 15%; then, the evaluator will conclude that the 8-point difference between programs is not significant from a practical perspective, although it is statistically significant.

Evaluation 2. Consider another evaluation with 15 of 25 students (60%) responding to a new elementary school science program and 13 of 25 (52%) to a traditional program. The sample size is $\frac{1}{32}$ of that in the first example. The p value is .57 in this evaluation, in contrast to $p = .001$ in the larger evaluation (see Figure 7.4). These p's correspond to the same observed 8-percentage-point difference. In this evaluation, the 95% CI extends from -19% to $+35\%$; these values are statistically indistinguishable from the observed difference of 8 percentage points. The larger evaluation permits a more precise estimate of the true value. The greater width of the interval also shows the greater uncertainty produced in an estimate based on a smaller sample. Thus, the use of a confidence interval enables the evaluator to assess statistical and practical or educational significance.

Ex.	% Responding		p value	Statistical Significance	Difference in % Responding		Graph of 95% CI (• = Point Estimate)	Practical Significance
	New	Standard			Point Estimate	95% CI		
1	480/800 = 60%	416/800 = 52%	0.001	Yes	8%	3% to 13%		No
2	15/25 = 60%	13/25 = 52%	0.57	No	8%	−19% to 35%		Inconclusive
3	15/25 = 60%	9/25 = 36%	0.09	No	24%	−3% to 51%		Inconclusive
4	240/400 = 60%	144/400 = 36%	< 0.0001	Yes	24%	17% to 31%		Yes

Graph axis: −20% −10% 0% 10% 20% 30% 40% 50%

Zero Difference

Smallest Practically Important Difference Assumed to Be 15%

Figure 7.4. Statistical Significance and Clinical Significance Using 95% Confidence Intervals (CI) of Differences Between Students in Two Programs

SOURCE: Reproduced with permission, from L. E. Braitman, Confidence Intervals Assess Both Clinical and Statistical Significance. *Annals of Internal Medicine*, 1991, 114: 515-517.

Guideline for Establishing Practical Significance

A difference in outcome between two groups in a program evaluation is significant in an educational sense when its 95% confidence interval is completely above the smallest practical or educationally important difference.

As can be seen from Figure 7.4, the confidence interval (3% to 13%) obtained for Evaluation 1 falls below the desired 15-point difference; it is not practically significant. The difference between groups obtained in Evaluation 2 (−19% to 35%) contains the smallest difference, so no definite conclusion about practical and educational significance is possible.

Evaluation 3. In this evaluation, 15 of 25 (60%) and 9 of 25 (36%) students benefit from the new and traditional programs. The confidence interval for the difference (60% − 36% = 24%) is −3% to 51% (see Figure 7.4). The *p* value (found in a table in a statistics text) is equal to or greater than .05, not statistically significant. The confidence interval and *p* are related; if the interval contains 0, then the *p* is not significant. In this case, 0% can be found in the −3% to 51% interval. But 0% is only one of many values inside the confidence interval. The evaluator cannot state, "There is no meaningful difference," because much of the interval falls above the 15-point difference cutoff. The results can be interpreted as practically or educationally inconclusive.

Evaluation 4. In this evaluation, 240 of 400 students (60%) respond to the new program, while 144 of 400 (36%) respond to the traditional or standard program. The difference is 24%; the 95% CI is

17% to 31% (see Figure 7.4). The difference is statistically ($p < .05$) and practically significant.

Screening and Transforming Data: Proceed With Caution

Before an evaluator analyzes data, the entire data set should be reviewed. A first step is to screen for outliers and incorrect values. **Outliers** are observations not consistent with the rest of the data set. For example, an outlier might consist of only 1 of 15 schools with uncharacteristically very low math scores. Including the school's data might bias the results, but excluding it might also do the same, and in addition the exclusion might be unethical. The evaluator who finds outliers in the data set could run the main analysis twice: with and without the outlier. In this way, the effects of the outlier can be determined and the results used in deciding how to handle the outlier.

Another step in reviewing an evaluation's data set is to screen it for incorrect values—that is, erroneous statistics. For example, if an evaluation of a program to improve the quality of art education for teens from low-income families has data on students who are 2 or 22 years of age, the ages may be errors in data entry.

A third step is to decide what to do about missing values. **Missing values** are data not collected from an individual or other sampling unit. Suppose an evaluator needed information on teachers' attitudes toward their working conditions. Suppose also that, of 100 teachers, only 75 respond to all questions on an attitude survey. If a complete set of information on all teachers is necessary for the analysis, then the evaluation's sample size must be treated as 75, and not as 100 respondents.

Another example of missing values is failure on the part of all or nearly all people to provide data on a variable. This can happen, for example, if nearly all teachers fail to answer one or more items on the survey of their attitudes. In this situation, the evaluator probably should exclude the items from the analysis.

Data also may need to be transformed or changed from one scale to another. **Linear transformations** are made for convenience and so that statistical methods based on a normal distribution can be used. Transformations involve a change in the mean and a scaling factor. This occurs, for example, when the z transformation is used and the mean of a distribution is expressed as 0 and its standard deviation (a measure of dispersion) is 1. **Nonlinear transformations** result in changing the shape of the distribution so that they become normal; statistical tests, like the t test, then can be used. With **rank transformations**, observations are rank-ordered from lowest to highest. The rank transformation is appropriate when observations are skewed.

The Codebook

The main purpose of preparing a codebook is to make a data set comprehensible to anyone who would like to use it. The codebook can be begun as soon as the analysis plan is agreed on (say, after the evaluator is sure of the evaluation questions and measures), but it should be made final after the completion of data screening and cleaning. Usually, the codebook contains a number for each variable, its location (the column in which it can be found), a name for the variable (of eight or fewer characters in capital letters to accommodate common statistical packages), and a brief description of the meaning of each code. Figure 7.5 is a portion of a codebook for a data set collected from a survey of students' self-confidence.

Reading Computer Output

Suppose an evaluator needs a chi-square analysis. Depending on the choice of statistical program, the output will contain the analysis *and* additional information. Computer printouts vary in how they present results and in the additional tests and data they provide. Evaluators should become multilingual so that they can adequately read and discuss a range of statistical programs. Practice helps, and

Variable Number	Variable Location (Column)	Variable Name	Description and Comments
1	1-5	PROJID	A 5-digit ID project code; use 99999 for missing values.
2	6-9	INDIVID	A 4-digit ID individual code: use 9999 for missing values.
3	10-15	PREDATE	Pretest date. Enter mo/day/yr using 2 digits for each segment. May 20, 1992 = 052092. Use 99 for any missing segment; use 999999 if entire date is missing.
4	16-21	POSTDATE	Posttest date. Use same procedure as for PREDATE.
5	22	GENDER	1 = Female; 2 = male; 9 = no data
6	23-24	AGE	Age in years at last birthday; 99 = no data
7	25	HNSTRMBL	Hands ever tremble when public speaking? 1 = no; 2 = yes; 9 = no data
8	26	SITSTILL	Ever have trouble sitting still? 1 = no; 2 = yes; 9 = no data

Figure 7.5. Portions of a Codebook

so, in the next sections, two commonly used statistical techniques are discussed and their corresponding outputs in one program application are illustrated.

CHI-SQUARE

The chi-square (χ^2) distribution is the most commonly used method of comparing proportions. It is represented by the Greek letter chi: χ.

Table 7.1. Comparing Program Participants in Their Preferences

| | *Marginal Frequencies* | | |
	Jobs Program	*No Program*	*Total*
Prefer college			40
Do not prefer college			168
Total	103	105	208

Table 7.2. No Relationship Between Program Participants and Nonparticipants in Their Preferences

| | *Expected Frequencies* | | |
	Jobs Program	*No Program*	*Total*
Prefer college	20	20	40
Do not prefer college	84	84	168
Total	104	104	208

Suppose you surveyed 208 high school seniors to determine their career preferences. Of the total, 103 have spent a year in a special jobs-training program; the others have not. The survey finds that 40 seniors prefer to go on to college before seeking employment, while the remainder prefer to enter the labor force immediately.

The questions you are interested in answering are:

1. Does a difference exist between program participants and the others in the number or proportion of seniors preferring to continue their education?
2. Does an association (or relationship) exist between being in the program and also preferring to continue in college?

To answer these questions, you could create a table that looks like Table 7.1.

The **marginal frequencies** represent the numbers or proportions of seniors in the two survey groups. The **expected frequencies**, shown in Table 7.2, represent the numbers or proportions of seniors in each cell, assuming no relationship (the null hypothesis) exists between preference and program participation.

Table 7.3.

	Experimental	Control	Total
Positive	a	b	a + b
Negative	c	d	c + d
Total	a + c	b + d	a + b + c + d = n

Expected frequencies refers to the hypothetical distribution if the views of the two groups being compared are alike. So, if 40 people prefer college, as the illustrative survey finds, then the expected frequency is 20 in the jobs program group and 20 in the group of nonparticipants.

Chi-square tests enable the comparison of the expected frequency in each cell with the frequency that actually occurs (observed frequencies). **Observed frequencies** refer to the survey's data. The differences between observed and expected frequencies are combined to form the chi-square statistic. If a relationship exists between the column and row variables (e.g., whether the person is in a program and his or her preference), the two are said to be dependent. In this case, you would decide in favor of differences between the groups.

To assist you in using chi-square tests with two groups (e.g., experimental and control) and a two-pronged dichotomous nominal survey outcome (e.g., yes, prefer college; or no, do not prefer college), use the notation shown in Table 7.3.

This is called a 2 × 2 table. The formula for calculating the chi-square for data in a 2 × 2 table is:

$$\chi^2 (1) = n(ad - bc)^2/(a + c)(b + d)(a + b)(c + d)$$

The (1) refers to the **degrees of freedom,** a parameter used also in the t distribution. A **parameter** is the population (as contrasted with a sample) value of a distribution (e.g., the mean of the population is mu [μ], and the standard deviation is sigma [σ]). The chi-square test is performed as a one-tailed test. If the observed frequencies depart from the expected frequencies by more than the amount that can be expected by chance, the null must be rejected.

Table 7.4.

	Jobs program	No program	Total
Prefer college	80	30	110
Do not prefer college	23	75	98
Total	103	105	208

Going back to the example of preference for college when comparing program and nonprogram participants, suppose the 2×2 table was filled out to look like Table 7.4. Using the formula, the following calculations would be done:

$$\chi^2 (1) = n(ad - bc)^2/(a + c)(b + d)(a + b)(c + d)$$

$$\chi^2 = \frac{208[(80)(75) - (30)(23)]^2}{(103)(105)(110)(98)}$$

$$\chi^2 = \frac{208(5310)^2}{116585700}$$

$$\chi^2 = 50.30$$

The critical value for an alpha of .01 is 6.635 according to the table for the chi-square distribution (found in statistics texts). In other words, 99% of the distribution is below 6.635. Any obtained value above the critical value enables the evaluator to reject the null hypothesis that no difference exists between the program and no program groups. In the example, the obtained statistic is above the critical value, and so the null hypothesis is rejected. The conclusion is that differences exist between the groups and that preference for college is related to program participation.

Chi-square tests can be performed with many numbers of columns and rows. Sometimes, chi-square values are "corrected," with a **continuity correction** or **Yates correction**. The correction involves subtracting 0.5 from the absolute value of $ad - bc$ before squaring. Its purpose is to lower the value of the obtained statistic, reducing the risk of a Type I error (rejecting the null when it is true); however, the risk of a Type II error (failing to reject the null when it is false) increases. Finally, when the expected frequencies are small (less than 5), then **Fisher's Exact Test** can be used. (For more information, consult the appropriate references at the end of the chapter.)

Example 7.3 shows a typical chi-square analysis.

Example 7.3. Reading Computer Output—Chi-Square

Background

Concern has been raised that graduates of the Self-Help Program, a 2-year work and study program, do not have adequate access to the social, educational, and health services they need. One important question is "Does a difference exist in health care use between program graduates who are employed and those who are unemployed? More specifically, does the proportion of graduates who have a paying job differ from the proportion who do not, in terms of whether or not they have seen any doctor (MD) more than once?"

Data Collection

Self-administered questionnaire with these questions:

1. In the past year, did you see any MD more than once? (yes or no)
2. In the past year, did you have a full- or part-time paying job that lasted 9 months or more? (yes or no)

Independent Variable

Job status (having a full- or part-time paying job or not having one)

Dependent Variable

Use of health services (seeing an MD more than once)

Analysis Method

Chi-square

Computer Output

Computer output for chi-square (see Figure 7.6)

Interpretation

a. Q41c refers to the question on the self-administered questionnaire that asks whether the graduate has seen any MD more than once.

b. Q61 refers to the question on the self-administered questionnaire that asks whether the graduate has a paying job.

c. Yes, the column that refers to the positive answer to the question about having a paying job

d. No, the column that refers to the negative answer to the question about having a paying job

e. Yes, the row that pertains to the positive answer to the question pertaining to seeing or not seeing any MD

f. No, the row that pertains to the negative answer to the question pertaining to seeing or not seeing any MD

g. The total number (855) and percentage (67.7) of graduates who saw an MD more than once

h. The total number (407) and percentage (32.3) of graduates who did not see an MD more than once

i. The total number (347) and percentage (27.5) of graduates who have a paying job

j. The total number (915) and percentage (72.5) of graduates who do not have a paying job

k. and l. The percentage of graduates that are represented in each cell. For example, in the top left cell (Cell a) are 224 graduates. They represent 26.2% of the 855 who saw any MD more than once and 64.6% of the 347 who also have a paying job.

m. The total number of graduates (1,262)

n. The value refers to the results of the statistical computation.

Pearson	6.32224	5	.27611
Likelihood Ratio	6.53980	5	.25718
Mantel-Haenszel test for linear association	.10445	1	.74656

Minimum Expected Frequency = 14.775

Number of Missing Observations: 18

Page 22   SPSS/PC+   6/24/93

Q41C[a]   SEE ANY MD MORE THAN ONCE by Q61[b] PAYING JOB

```
              Q61              Page 1 of 1
         Count    o
         Row Pct  o YES c   NO d
         Col Pct  o                      Row
                  o  1.00  o   2.00  o  Total
Q41C     ááááááááéáááááááááéáááááááááéáááááÇ
         1.00  o   224   o   631   o  855 g
YES e          o   26.2  o   73.8  o  67.7
               o   64.6  o   69.0  o
               ûááááááááéáááááááááéáááááÇ
         2.00  o   123   o   284   o  407 h
NO f           o   30.2 k o  69.8 k o  32.3
               o   35.4 l o  31.0 l o
               ááááááááéáááááááááéáááááí
         Column    347 i     915 j    1262 m
         Total     27.5      72.5     100.0
```

Page 23   SPSS/PC+ [n]   6/24/93 [p]

Chi-Square	Value	DF [o]	Significance
Pearson [q]	2.23778	1	.13467
Continuity Correction [r]	2.04057	1	.15315
Likelihood Ratio [s]	2.21574	1	.13661
Mantel-Haenszel test for [t] linear association	2.23601	1	.13483

Minimum Expected Frequency [u] = 111.909

Figure 7.6. Computer Output—Chi-Square

o. The degrees of freedom

p. The obtained *p* value. This value is compared to alpha. If it is less, the null is rejected.

q. Pearson is the particular type of chi-square statistic calculated by this particular statistical package.

r. Continuity correction involves subtracting .05 from the difference between observed and expected frequencies before squaring to make the chi-square value smaller.

s. The likelihood ratio is the odds that the results occur in graduates who have seen any MD more than once versus those who have not.

t. Mantel-Haenszel test for linear association is a logrank test for comparing two survival distributions (see the appropriate suggested reading at end of chapter for more information).

u. Minimum expected frequency will tell whether you have enough to proceed with the chi-square test or whether you should consider Fisher's Exact Test.

Conclusion

The obtained significance level is .13467. The null hypothesis (no differences exist between graduates with and without paying jobs and whether or not they saw any MD) is retained.

---

t TEST

The *t* distribution is a probability distribution similar to the standard normal distribution, or *z*. It is used to test hypotheses about means (and thus requires numerical data). The shape of a *t* distribution approaches the shape of a standard normal distribution as the sample size and degrees of freedom increase. In fact, when the sample has 30 or more graduates, the two curves are very similar, and either distribution can be used to answer statistical questions. Current practice in most fields, however, relies on the *t* distribution even with large sample sizes.

Three situations can arise in which *t* tests are appropriate, as illustrated in Example 7.4.

Example 7.4. Three Situations and the *t* Test

Situation 1: Children's Birthday Gifts

Children in McCarthy Elementary School received an average of 4.2 birthday gifts. How does this compare with the results obtained in the national survey of children and birthday gifts?

Type of t: One-sample *t*

Comment: The mean of a group is compared with a *norm,* or standard value (the results of the national survey)

Situation 2: A Low-Fat Diet for Students

Do average scores on the Feel Good Inventory change for students after they participate in the Low Fat Diet Program?

Type of t: Dependent *t*

Comment: The mean of a single group is compared at two times (before and after participation in the Low Fat Diet Program).

Situation 3: Learning Ballet

On average, how do boys and girls compare in their attitudes toward ballet after participation in the Ballet Exercise Program? The highest possible score is 50 points.

Type of t: Independent *t*

Comment: The means of two independent groups are compared.

To apply the *t* test appropriately, data must meet certain assumptions. To use the *t* distribution for one mean (as in Situation 1), the assumption is that the observations (e.g., scores) are normally distributed. Some computer programs provide a probability plot that will enable you to certify that the data are consistent with this assumption. Sometimes, you can examine the distribution yourself by plotting the data as a histogram or box-and-whisker plot. If the data are not normally distributed, they can be transformed into a normal distribution. Alternatively, you may decide not to use the *t*, and instead use different statistical measures called **nonparametric procedures** to analyze the data. Nonparametric methods make no assumptions about the distribution of observed values.

A paired design is used to detect the difference between the means obtained by the same group, usually measured twice (as in Situation 2 above). With the paired *t*, the assumption is that the observations are distributed normally. If the data violate the assumption, a commonly used nonparametric test for the difference between two paired samples is the **Wilcoxon Signed-Ranks Test**. This method tests the hypothesis that the medians, rather than the means, are equal.

The *t* test for independent groups (Situation 3 above) assumes that the observations are normally distributed and that the variances of the observations are equal. If the sample sizes are equal, unequal variances will not have a major effect on the significance level of the test. If they are not equal, a downward adjustment of the degrees of freedom is made (you have fewer), and separate variance estimates are used instead of the combined or "pooled" variance. The statistical test to compare variances is the *F* test; many computer programs perform the *F* test, often in the same program that performs the *t* test. If one of the assumptions of the independent *t* test is violated, an alternative is the nonparametric **Wilcoxon Rank-Sum Test** (the Mann-Whitney *U*). This test assesses the equality of medians, rather than of means (as does the Wilcoxon Signed Ranks Test).

Figure 7.7 contains a sample computer printout for a *t* test from SPSS-PC+; it is explained in Example 7.5.

Example 7.5. Reading Computer Output—Independent Samples *t* Test

Background

School District A's planners are concerned that families with the sickest children are not sending them as often as they should to the People's Ambulatory Care Clinic (PACE), a school-based health care center. PACE receives much of its support from the Williamson Foundation. A group of families is being compared with a control to look at use of services and outcomes. If the evaluation reveals underuse of services by experimental families, the clinic is in danger of losing its financial support from the foundation.

Data Collection

1. Self-administered questionnaire with this question:

   In the past year, did your child see any MD in the clinic more than once? (yes or no)

2. The Instrumental Activities of Living (IADL). This measure has 20 questions about children's health status. A score of 100 represents optimal health status.

Independent Variable

Use of health services (seeing an MD more than once at PACE or not)

Dependent Variable

Health status: Score on the IADL

Analysis Method

t test

Computer Output

Computer output for *t* test (see Figure 7.7)

Page 97 SPSS/PC+ 6/23/93
Independent samples of Q41D — SEE MD AT PACE CLINIC > 1 TIME
a *b*
Group 1: Q41 EQ 1.00 Group 2: Q41 EQ 2.00

t-test for: IADL

	c Number of Cases	*d* Mean	*e* Standard Deviation	*f* Standard Error
Group 1	561	75.5246	23.957	1.011
Group 2	311	77.4358	24.112	1.367

		∘	*i* Pooled Variance Estimate		∘	*j* Separate Variance Estimate		
g	*h*	∘			∘			
F	2-Tail	∘	t	Degrees of	2-Tail	∘	t	Degrees of	2-Tail
Value	Prob.	∘	Value	Freedom	Prob.	∘	Value	Freedom	Prob.
1.01	.890		−1.13	870	.261		−1.12	636.61	.262

Figure 7.7. Computer Output—*t* Test

Interpretation

a. Group 1 answered yes to the question: Did you or your child see an MD at the PACE clinic more than once this year? The choices were: 1 = yes; 2 = no.

b. Group 2 answered no to the question: Did you or your child see an MD at the PACE clinic more than once this year?

c. Number of Cases refers to the number of children (sample size) in each group.

d. The mean score obtained on the IADL by each group

e. The standard deviation of the scores

f. The standard error of the means

g. The *F* value or statistic obtained in the test to determine the equality of the variances

h. The probability of obtaining a result like the F value if the null is true. If the obtained probability is less than some agreed-on alpha, such as .05 or. 01, the null is rejected. In this case, the probability of .890 is greater than .05, and so the null is retained. The conclusion is that no differences exist in the variances of the two groups.

i. The pooled variance estimate is used when variances are equal. The p value is .261, greater than an alpha of .05. The null hypothesis regarding the equality of the group means is retained.

j. The separate variance is used when variances are not equal.

Conclusion

No differences exist in health status between children who saw a doctor at the PACE clinic more than one time and those who did not.

Meta-Analysis:
A Super Analysis of Evaluation Data

A **meta-analysis** is a method for combining studies that address the same research questions. The idea is that the larger numbers obtained from contributing studies have greater statistical power and generalizability together than any of the individual studies. Meta-analyses provide a quantitative alternative to the traditional review article in which experts use judgment and intuition to reach conclusions about the merits of a treatment or program or, alternatively, base their conclusions on a count of the number of positive versus negative and inconclusive studies.

Suppose a meta-analysis is to be conducted to answer the question "Does the Health Assessment and Prevention Program for Youth (HAPPY) result in improved health habits?" To answer the question, the evaluator completes these tasks:

A Guide to the Tasks Required
to Conduct a Meta-Analysis

1. State the problem—in this case, whether HAPPY improves teen health habits.
2. Identify all studies that address the problem.
3. Prepare a scale to rate the quality of the studies.
4. Have at least two people review and rate the quality.
5. Include all studies that meet the criteria for quality, according to the reviewer's ratings of quality.
6. The difference in improvement between adolescents who were educated and those who were not is calculated and is plotted as a point on a chart.
7. The chances that the study can be repeated and produce the same results are calculated; the statistical range shows up as a line on the chart. Figure 7.8 shows how the meta-analysis turned out.

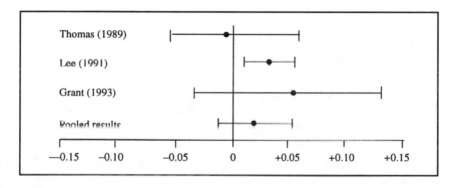

Figure 7.8. Meta-Analysis of Educational Programs for Adolescent Health Care

These three hypothetical evaluations show that the weight of the results suggests that programs to educate teens to improve health habits have no advantage over the controls.

The methods of meta-analysis are continually advancing. Meta-analyses have not been used to combine the results of program evaluations because too few scientifically appropriate studies have been conducted on any single topic to make the effort worthwhile. Nevertheless, familiarity with the tasks included in a meta-analysis is important because evaluators may need to perform many, if not all, of them and to review and use the results. All meta-analyses require a review of the literature to identify eligible studies, preparation and use of a measure of the quality of the literature, selection of studies for the meta-analysis, and performance of the analysis and interpretation of the results. At the minimum, evaluators must be able to review the literature in a systematic fashion because data from published and unpublished sources are used to help set standards of program performance; determine sample size; provide paradigms of research design, measurement, data analysis, and presentation; explain the context in which the present evaluation is conducted; and demonstrate how the present evaluation's findings will add to current knowledge.

SUMMARY AND TRANSITION TO NEXT CHAPTER ON EVALUATION REPORTS

This chapter discussed the types of analysis that are particularly useful in program evaluations. Before choosing a method of analysis, the evaluator should determine the number of variables and the characteristics of the data describing or measuring each: nominal, ordinal, or numerical. When using tests of significance, the evaluator should decide on educational, as well as statistical, meaning.

The next chapter discusses written and oral reports. It addresses the contents of written reports, including the objectives, methods, results, conclusions, discussion, and recommendations. Special emphasis is placed on the use of tables and figures to present data. The chapter also explains the contents of an abstract. Because much of evaluation reporting is oral, the chapter provides guidelines for the preparation of visual aids, such as overhead transparencies and slides.

EXERCISES:
ANALYZING EVALUATION DATA

Directions

1. For each of the following situations, describe the independent and dependent variables and tell whether they will be described with nominal, ordinal, or numerical data.

Situation	*Describe Independent and Dependent Variables*	*Tell Whether the Data Are Nominal, Ordinal, or Numerical*
Children in the experimental and control groups are tested to determine whether their reading ability improved, remained the same, or worsened.		
Participants in the program are grouped according to whether they are severely, moderately, or marginally depressed and are given a survey of anxiety that is scored from 1 to 9.		
Children are chosen for the evaluation according to whether they have had all recommended vaccinations or not; they are followed for 5 years.		

Situation	Describe Independent and Dependent Variables	Tell Whether the Data Are Nominal, Ordinal, or Numerical
Boys and girls from higher and lower income families are compared in the quality of their lives as measured by scores ranging from 1 to 50 that are obtained from standardized observations.		
Instructors and supervisors are surveyed, and their average scores are compared.		

2. Use the following information to select and justify a method of data analysis.

Evaluation question: After program participation, is domestic violence decreased?

Standard: A statistically significant difference in domestic violence is found in families that have participated in the experimental program, as compared with the control program.

Independent variable: Group membership (experimental vs. control)

Design: An experimental design with concurrent controls

Sampling: Eligible participants are assigned at random to an experimental and control group. Each group has 100 participants (a statistically derived sample size).

Dependent variable: Domestic violence

Types of data: Data on domestic violence will come from the DONT Survey, a 50-point measure in which lower scores mean less violence.

3. Suppose the evaluation of the program to reduce domestic violence is concerned with finding out how younger and older persons compare in the experimental and control groups. Assuming the use of the DONT Survey, which produces numerical scores, which statistical method would be appropriate? Explain.

Suggested Readings

Afifi, A. A., & Clark, V. (1990). *Computer-aided multivariate analysis.* New York: Van Nostrand Reinhold.

A textbook on multivariate analysis with a practical approach. Discusses data entry, data screening, data reduction, and data analysis. Also explains the options available in different statistical packages.

Braitman, L. E. (1991). Confidence intervals assess both clinical and statistical significance. *Annals of Internal Medicine, 114,* 515-517.

Contains one of the clearest explanations anywhere of the use of confidence intervals and is highly recommended.

Dawson-Saunders, B., & Trapp, R. (1994). *Basic and clinical biostatistics* (2nd ed.). Norwalk, CT: Appleton & Lange.

An excellent biostatistics text.

Goldstein, H. (1987). *Multilevel models in educational and social research.* London: Oxford University Press.

An advanced book covering such topics as the basic multilevel linear model, general multilevel linear model with random coefficients, longitudinal and repeated measures data, and proportions as responses.

Jaeger, R. M. (1991). *Statistics: A spectator sport.* Newbury Park, CA: Sage.

A relatively easy-to-follow book that is a very fine introduction to basic analytic tools, such as concepts of central tendency, variability, and correlation. Other issues worth reading about are the logic of hypothesis testing and fundamentals of measurement (including reliability and validity).

Norusis, M. J. (1983). *SPSS introductory statistics guide.* Chicago: SPSS.

This manual accompanies a statistical package for the social sciences. It contains an overview and explanation of the logic behind most of the statistical methods commonly used in the social sciences. The manual also presents and explains statistical output.

Siegel, S. (1956). *Nonparametric statistics for the behavioral sciences.* New York: McGraw-Hill.

A classic textbook on nonparametric statistics.

Wiersma, W. (1991). *Research methods in education* (5th ed.). Boston: Allyn & Bacon.

Provides very good explanations of the methods that should be used to conduct research in education.

Review Notes

Purpose of This Chapter

This chapter focuses on the evaluation report. A report of a completed evaluation answers the evaluation questions, describes how the answers were obtained, and translates the findings into conclusions and recommendations about the program and the evaluation.

Evaluation reports can be written and oral. The chapter first discusses how to prepare a written report of an evaluation and provides a checklist and scoring sheet for assessing its quality. Figures and tables are used to present evaluation results, and these also are discussed.

The oral presentation is examined next. Emphasis is on preparing visuals (e.g., overhead transparencies and slides) for 10-minute to 60-minute talks.

 **Evaluation Reports**

The Written Evaluation Report

A written report is required of nearly all evaluations. A useful report provides enough information so that at least two interested individuals can agree on the evaluation's purposes, methods, and conclusions. If the report is to be submitted to a funding agency, such as a foundation or the government, the composition and format of the report may be set for you. In most cases, however, evaluators are on their own in deciding on the length and content of the report.

LENGTH

The text of an evaluation report should be between 5,000 and 15,000 words, or 20 to 60 double-spaced pages (with standard 10- or 12-pitch type, 12-pitch spacing, and 1-inch margins). A list of bibliographic references should accompany the report. Up to 10 tables and 10 figures (e.g., photographs, graphs) should be adequate. In addition, an abstract of 250 words and a summary of up to 15 pages are often helpful. In the appendix to the report, the evaluator can put working documents, such as resumes, project worksheets, survey response frequencies, complex mathematical calculations, copies of measures (e.g., questionnaire surveys, record review forms), organizational charts, memorandums, training materials, and project planning documents. Including the appendix, the evaluation report can be hundreds of pages.

Consider this ideal table of contents for a report of a 10th-grade social and political science program (Example 8.1).

Example 8.1. Sample Table of Contents for a Report: An Evaluation of Modern Political and Social Studies (MOPSS) Program

Abstract: 250 words
Summary: 8 pages
Text of Report: 41 pages

I. Introduction: The need for the program and a brief description of the program and the evaluation questions (6 pages)

II. Methods (10 pages)

   A. Evaluation Design

   B. Objectives and Activities of the Intervention and Control Programs

   C. Sample

      1. Inclusion and exclusion criteria

      2. Justification of sample sizes

      3. How sample was selected and assigned to groups

   D. Outcome Measures

      1. Reliability and validity of measures of knowledge, attitude, and performance

      2. Quality assurance system for the data collection

   E. Analysis

      Citing and (justifying) the specific method used to test each hypothesis or to answer each evaluation question

III. Results (15 pages)

   A. Response rates

   B. Demographic and other descriptive characteristics

   C. Knowledge

   D. Attitudes

   E. Behavior

   F. Costs

   G. Program Activities and Outcomes

IV. Conclusions (8 pages)

V. Recommendations (2 pages)

VI. Tables and Figure

   A. Table 1. Demographic Characteristics of Participants

   B. Table 2. Comparison Between Experimental and Control Groups: Knowledge, Attitude, Behavior

C. Table 3. Comparative Costs

D. Table 4. Program Activities as Predictors of Performance

E. Figure 1. Flow chart: How participants were assigned to groups by "cluster"

VII. Appendixes

A. Copies of all measures

B. Calculations linking costs and effectiveness

C. Final sample size calculations

D. Testimony from students, parents, and teachers regarding their satisfaction with participation in the experimental program

E. Informed consent statements

F. List of expert panel participants and affiliations

G. Training materials for all data collection

H. Data collection quality assurance plan

CONTENTS

Introduction

The introduction to an evaluation report has three components: (a) a problem that needs to be resolved, (b) an explanation of the means by which the experimental program is to solve the problem, and (c) a list of questions the evaluation answers about the merits of the program's solution to the problem. Example 8.2 illustrates the contents of the introduction to a written report pertaining to an evaluation of a program in education.

Example 8.2. What to Include in the Introduction to a Written Report

1. *The Problem.* Describe the problem that the program and its evaluation are designed to solve. In the description, tell how many students, teachers, schools, and so forth are affected by the problem and what its human and financial costs are. Cite the literature to defend the estimates of the importance and costs of the problem.

2. *The Program.* Give an overview of the program's objectives and activities and any unique features (e.g., its size, location, or number and types of participants). If the program has been modeled on some other intervention, describe the similarities and differences and cite references.

3. *The Evaluation.* Give the objectives of the evaluation and state the questions and standards. Establish the connections between the general problem, the objectives of the program, and the evaluation; that is, tell how the evaluation will provide knowledge about this particular program and also advance knowledge about the problem, as in this example:

Sample Introduction

This evaluation studied the effectiveness of Modern Political and Social Studies (MOPSS), a curriculum for high school students. The program's main goal is to foster the knowledge, attitudes, and behaviors needed by young people to fully participate in a pluralistic, democratic society.

MOPSS was developed in response to mounting evidence [references should be given here] that high school students in Hypothetical School District have inadequate knowledge and understanding of the foundations of democracy. On standardized tests, the district's students performed below state and national levels when confronted with questions pertaining to the Constitution, the legal system, and voting rights and responsibilities. (The Appendix contains the distribution of scores.)

The relatively poor performance is probably the result of many causes. A districtwide survey (see the Appendix) revealed that over 50% of parents and 75% of students agreed that a watered-down political and social studies curriculum is definitely or probably a major contributing factor.

MOPSS is a 1-year program involving an interdisciplinary team of teachers. It relies on college-based techniques such as seminars and small-group discussions. Instructional materials are diverse and include conventional textbooks, video, and so on.

Schools were randomly assigned to MOPSS or their traditional program. The evaluation focused on determining the extent to which the program achieved its specific goals and objectives, the relationship among program activities and outcomes, and the comparative costs of MOPSS and the traditional program.

Methods

The methods section of the report should describe the program, define terms, and describe the design, sample, measures, and analysis.

The Program. Describe the experimental and comparison programs. Carefully distinguish between them. For how long did each participate in the evaluation? If program implementation was standardized, describe how and discuss any training that occurred.

Definitions. Define all potentially ambiguous terms. When appropriate, distinguish between practical and statistical significance for the main outcome measures.

Design. Tell whether the evaluation used an experimental or observational design. If the design was experimental, give the type (e.g., concurrent controls in which participants are randomly assigned to experimental and control groups).

Sample. Give the inclusion and exclusion criteria for participation in the evaluation. Tell whether the participants were randomly selected and randomly assigned. Explain how the sample sizes were determined.

Measures. Describe the characteristics of each measure of the main evaluation questions. Who administered the measure? Was training required? Is the measure reliable? valid? How much time is required to complete the measure? How many questions does it contain? How were they selected? If appropriate, cite the theory behind the choice of questions or the other measures on which they were based. How was the measure scored?

Analysis. Check each evaluation question for the main variables. Then, for the main variables, describe and justify the analytic method. Were any unusual methods used in the analysis? If yes, these should be described. Name the statistical package in case other evaluators want to perform a similar analysis using the same setup. If a relatively new or complex data-analytic method was used, provide a reference for it.

Results

Present the results of the statistical analyses. Give all response rates and describe the evaluation participants' characteristics. When appropriate, compare the sample who agreed to participate with those who refused or did not complete the entire program or provide complete data. Give the results for each major evaluation question and its subquestions. For example, if a main question asks whether students' knowledge improves, present the results for that question; when helpful, also provide data on types of individuals (e.g., 10th graders? 11th? 12th? boys? girls? students planning to enter 4-year colleges?) for whom the program was most and least effective.

Use tables and graphs to summarize the results. Example 8.3 contains a table suitable for evaluation reports.

Example 8.3. A Table to Describe the Characteristics of an Evaluation's Participants

Characteristic	Experimental		Control		Difference	Confidence Interval*
	n	(%)	n	(%)		
Age, y						
Under 14						
15-16						
Over 16						
Grade point average (4 = highest; 1 = lowest)						
3.5-4.0						
3.0-3.4						
2.0-2.9						
1.9 or less						
Number of years living in the district						
More than 5						
3 to 5						
1 or 2						
Less than 1						

NOTE: *A *confidence interval* refers to the interval computed from sample data that has a given probability (e.g., 90% or 95%) that the unknown parameter (e.g., the difference) is contained within the interval. Suppose that the experimental group had an average grade point average of 2.8 and that the control had 1.4. The difference between the two is 1.4. If the 90% confidence limits were 1.0 and 3.1, the interval would be 3.1 minus 1.0, or 2.1. This means you can be 90% confident that the true difference between the two groups falls in the interval. You must be concerned about true differences when you sample because sampling is always an approximation of the truth.

Do *not* interpret data in the results section. Such statements as "These results contradict the findings of previous evaluations" belong in the discussion section.

Following are guidelines for the use of figures and tables.

Guidelines for Composing Figures and Tables in Evaluation Reports

Using Figures

Figure 8.1 shows the results of an evaluation of the Health Assessment and Prevention Program for Youth (HAPPY), a teacher-directed curriculum to improve the health-related knowledge and behavior of high school students. The figure reveals that, when compared with a control, HAPPY had its greatest effects on encouraging students to eat primarily vegetarian food and in maintaining better eating habits.

The figure conforms to these rules:

1. Place variables (in this case, experimental and control groups) that are being compared along the *x*-axis.
2. Place numbers along the *y* axis; when appropriate, include percentages on the figure.
3. Make sure that visual differences correspond to meaningful differences.
4. Include an explanation of the findings (e.g., results of chi-square tests).
5. Include a legend or key (e.g, darker shading is HAPPY; lighter shading is the control).

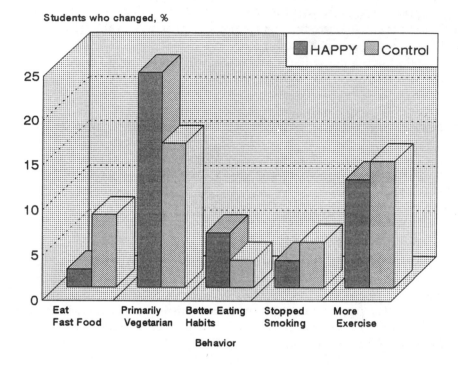

Figure 8.1. Health Promotion-Related Behavior Change From Baseline to Follow-Up

NOTE: Results of chi-square tests for each behavior were $p < .05$ for eating fast foods; $p < .05$ for primarily vegetarian; $p < .05$ for better eating habits; $p < .10$ for stopped smoking; and $p < .60$ for more exercise.

Using Tables

1. Put the most important values to be compared in columns. If you are describing the characteristics (e.g., age, educational level) of supporters and opponents of a proposed school bond (Figure 8.2), the values (e.g., numbers and percentages of persons with the differing characteristics) go in the columns.

2. If appropriate and possible, put statistical values in ascending (largest values) to descending (smallest values) order. Suppose Figure 8.3

Characteristics	Supporters N (%)	Opponents N (%)
Age, *y*		
18-21		
22-25		
26-35		
36-45		
46 and over		
Sex		
Male		
Female		
Years living in county		
Less than 1		
1-3		
4-6		
over 6		

Figure 8.2. The Columns: Supporters and Opponents of School Bond A

	Number of Children Choosing		
Region	Hot	Cold	Total
Northeast	140	124	264
South	100	52†	152
West	89	138‡	227
North Central	45	46	91
Total	374	360	734

Figure 8.3. Statistical Values in Order: The National Lunch Preference Survey

NOTE: Survey administered by the Center for Children's Choices, Washington DC.
† $p = .003$; ‡ $p = .002$

describes the results of a nationwide survey of 734 elementary school children who were asked whether or not they preferred hot or cold lunches.

Note that, in this figure, the preferences for hot lunches are in descending order. The choice of which values to place first depends on the points being emphasized. If the evaluation's focus was on preferences for cold lunches, then the first cell of the table under Region would have been West.

3. Use a standardized method for calling the reader's attention to key aspects of the table, such as statistical significance. For example, *, †, ‡, §, ¶ are one typical hierarchy.

Conclusions or Discussion

Tell what the results mean by answering questions like these:

1. Taking the broadest perspective, what can you conclude from the evaluation? Is the program any good? For whom? Under what circumstances?
2. Did the program achieve its goals and objectives?
3. For which participants was the program most effective?
4. For which participants was the program least effective?
5. Which components of the program were most/least effective?
6. How do the results of this evaluation compare in whole or in part to the findings of other studies?
7. What new knowledge about education, psychology, program evaluation, policy, and the system can be learned from this evaluation?
8. What gaps in knowledge have been revealed by this evaluation?
9. What are the limitations (due to imperfections in the design, sample, measurement, and analysis), and how do these affect the conclusions?

Recommendations

When making recommendations, consider answering questions like these:

1. Without changing its basic goals and objectives, if the program were to be redone to remove its flaws, what are the top five changes or additions that should be considered?

2. If the program were to be applied to another setting or group of participants, who is likely to benefit most?

3. If the program were to be instituted in the same or some other setting, what are the costs to expect?

4. What objectives should be changed or added to the program to expand its scope and effectiveness?

THE ABSTRACT

The abstract of an evaluation report is usually between 200 and 300 words. Its purpose is to present the evaluation's main objectives, methods, and findings. The following topics must be considered when writing the abstract, although the amount of detail will vary.

Objective: In one or two sentences, tell the purpose of the evaluation.

Design: Using a standard term, name the design. Use terms like *randomized controlled* [true experiment] or *nonrandomized* [quasi experiment] or *survey.*

Participants: Describe the characteristics of the participants, including the number of participants in the experimental and control groups; demographics (e.g., age, grade level, family income); region of the country; and size (e.g., number of students, teachers, ratio of teachers to students).

Main outcome measures: For each dependent variable in the evaluation question, describe the surveys, record reviews, tests, and observations that were used. Describe any unique features of the measures and include any special notes on reliability or validity.

Results: For each major dependent variable, give the results.

Conclusions: In one or two sentences explain what the results mean. Did the program work? Is it applicable to other participants?

Guidelines for Reviewing the Quality of the Report

After completing an evaluation report, it should be reviewed to determine the extent to which it conforms to acceptable standards. The following "scoring" sheet (Figure 8.4) is provided as a guide. It can be used also to review a variety of evaluation manuscripts and reports.

Scale: 4 = definitely yes
          3 = probably yes
          2 = probably no
          1 = definitely no
          0 = no data; uncertain
          NA = not applicable

CRITERIA: PRECISION OF OBJECTIVES, JUSTIFICATION OF STANDARDS	Rating Scale					
	4	3	2	1	0	NA
Are the evaluation's objectives/questions/hypotheses stated precisely?						
Are the standards clear?						
Are educational standards justified?						
Are statistical standards justified?						
Other?						

Figure 8.4. Reviewing Evaluations: A Scoring Guide

CRITERIA: NEED FOR THE EVALUATION	*Rating Scale*					
	4	3	2	1	0	NA
Is the evaluation justified?						
Is the present evaluation placed within the context of previous work?						
Are criteria given for any literature that is reviewed?						
Is the quality of the reviewed literature assessed?						
Does the present evaluation continue the work of others?						
Does the present evaluation build on the previous work of others?						
Does the present evaluation fill in gaps in knowledge?						
Other?						

CRITERIA: DESCRIPTION OF THE INTERVENTION	*Rating Scale*					
	4	3	2	1	0	NA
Is the importance of the problem to be solved by the program justified?						
Are experimental program goals and objectives specified?						
Are descriptions given of the special features of the experimental program?						
Are quality assurance systems in place for monitoring the implementation of the experimental program?						
Is the experimental program standardized within sites?						

Figure 8.4. (Continued)

CRITERIA: DESCRIPTION OF THE INTERVENTION	Rating Scale					
	4	3	2	1	0	NA
Is the experimental program standardized across sites?						
Are the resources of the experimental program described?						
Are the settings in which the experimental program takes place described?						
Are control group program goals and objectives specified?						
Are descriptions given of the implementation of the control group program?						
Are quality assurance systems in place for monitoring the implementation of the control group program?						
Is the control group program standardized within sites?						
Is the control group program standardized across sites?						
Are the resources of the control program described?						
Are the settings in which the control program takes place described?						
Are the effects on the evaluation's generalizability given for failure to have uniform program goals, objectives, protocols, settings, or resources?						
Other?						

Figure 8.4. (Continued)

CRITERIA: EVALUATION DESIGN AND SAMPLING	Rating Scale					
	4	3	2	1	0	NA
Is the entire population included?						
If a sample, are sampling methods adequately described?						
If a sample, are the evaluation's participants randomly selected?						
If more than one group, are the evaluation's participants randomly assigned?						
If the unit that is sampled (e.g., students) is not the population of main concern (e.g., teachers are), is this properly addressed in the analysis or discussion?						
If a sample, and a nonrandom sampling method is used, is evidence given regarding the similarity of the groups at baseline?						
If groups are not equivalent at baseline, is this problem adequately addressed in analysis or interpretation?						
Are criteria given for including all evaluation units (e.g., students, teachers, classes, schools)?						
Are criteria given for excluding evaluation units?						
Is the sample size justified (say, with a power calculation)?						
Is information given on the number of participants in the source population?						
Is information given on the number of participants eligible to participate?						

Figure 8.4. (Continued)

CRITERIA: EVALUATION DESIGN AND SAMPLING	Rating Scale					
	4	3	2	1	0	NA
Is information given on the number who agreed to participate?						
Is information given on the number who refused to participate?						
Is information given on the number who dropped out or were lost to follow-up before completing all elements of data collection?						
Is information given on the number who completed all elements of data collection?						
Is information given on the number on whom some data are missing?						
Are participants measured over time?						
If observations or measures are made over time, is the time period justified?						
Are participants blinded?						
Are reasons given for individuals or groups who dropped out?						
Are reasons given for missing data?						
Are the effects on generalizability of choice, equivalence, and participation of the resultant sample explained?						
Are the effects on internal validity of choice, equivalence, and participation of the resultant sample explained?						
Other?						

Figure 8.4. (Continued)

CRITERIA: JUSTIFICATION FOR AND VALIDITY OF DATA SOURCES AND DATA COLLECTION	Rating Scale					
	4	3	2	1	0	NA
Are the independent variables defined?						
Are the dependent variables defined?						
Are data provided on the reliability of data sources for the main variables?						
Are data provided on the validity of data sources for the main variables?						
Is the reliability of each data source adequate?						
Is the validity of each data source adequate?						
Are the data collection methods adequately described?						
Is information provided on methods for ensuring the quality of data collection?						
Is the length of the data collection period justified?						
Is the length of the data collection period sufficient for the evaluation's objectives?						
Are the effects on the evaluation's generalizability of the selection, reliability, validity of data sources, and length of data collection explained?						
Other?						

Figure 8.4. (Continued)

CRITERIA: APPROPRIATENESS OF DATA ANALYSIS	Rating Scale					
	4	3	2	1	0	NA
Are statistical methods adequately described?						
Are statistical methods justified?						
Is the purpose of the analysis clear?						
Are scoring systems described?						
Are potential confounders adequately controlled for in the analysis?						
Are the analytic specifications of the independent and dependent variables consistent with the evaluation questions or hypotheses under study?						
Is the unit of analysis specified clearly?						
Is a sensitivity analysis performed to account for imprecise measurements or uncertain outcomes?						
Other?						
CRITERIA: COMPLETENESS AND ACCURACY OF REPORTING	Rating Scale					
	4	3	2	1	0	NA
Are references given for complex statistical methods?						
Are complex statistical methods described in an appendix?						
Are exact p values given?						
Are confidence intervals given?						
Are the results of the analysis clearly described?						
Are the evaluation's results clearly described?						
Do the conclusions follow from the study's results?						
Other?						

Figure 8.4. (Continued)

CRITERIA: BOUNDARIES OF THE EVALUATION	*Rating Scale*					
	4	3	2	1	0	NA
Are the evaluation's biases explained?						
Are the results practical?						
Are the uses of the evaluation's findings clear?						
Are directives given for future evaluations?						
Are directives given for policy decisions?						
Are ethical considerations included?						
Other?						

Figure 8.4. (Continued)

The Oral Report

An oral report of a program evaluation may consist of an account of some or all of its objectives, methods, and findings. All reports can be reinforced by providing listeners with visual aids. The most common of these are slides and overhead transparencies. Slides are more expensive to produce than overheads and take more time to produce. As modes of presentation, slides have the reputation of being more "polished," but the comparative effectiveness of the two has not been evaluated.

The following guidelines can help in the preparation of 10-minute to 60-minute oral presentations in which slides or overheads are used to complement the evaluator's report.

Guidelines for the Preparation of
an Oral Program Evaluation Report

1. *Do the talking and explaining and let the audience listen.* Use visuals to focus the audience's attention on the key points of the talk. Do not require listeners to read and listen at the same time.

Poor:

Box 8.1. Reliability

A reliable measure is one that is relatively free from measurement error. Because of this error, individuals' obtained scores are different from their true scores. In some cases, the error results from the measure itself: It may be difficult to understand or poorly administered.

Better:

Box 8.2. Reliability

♦ Reliable measures are relatively free of error
♦ Causes of measurement error
  • Measure is hard to understand
  • Measure is poorly administered

Box 8.2 is better than Box 8.1 because the listener can more easily keep the main points in view without being diverted by the first visual's reading requirements. If the objective is to have the audience read something, then a handout (with time out for reading) is more appropriate than a visual.

2. *Each visual aid should have a title.*

3. *During the talk, address the talk's purposes and the evaluations's purposes, main methods, main results, conclusions, and recommendations.* A typical oral evaluation report covers the following:

A. *Title of the talk and names and affiliations of the evaluators:*

Box 8.3. Children and Reading: What the Evaluation Found

Prepared by:

Jane Austen, M.A.
Oliver Goldsmith, Ed.D.

The Center for Program Evaluation

B. *What the evaluation is about*

Box 8.4. Goal of the Evaluation of Children and Reading Program (CARP)

- To appraise impact
- To determine costs
- To estimate benefits

C. *The purpose of the report*

Box 8.5. Purpose

Describe and compare program children with other children in:

- Ability to read
- Attitude toward teaching

D. *A description of the program*

Box 8.6. The Children and Reading Program

- Goals are to foster love of reading and ability to read
- Begin education as early as 4 years of age
- 3-year program
- $3 million
- Sponsored by Education Trustees, a nonprofit philanthropic foundation

---

E. *A description of the participants*

Box 8.7. Who Was in CARP?

- 500 children between 4 and 7 years
- Six public schools: three in the experiment and three in the control
- Assignment of schools to groups was random
- Control schools have regular activities

F. *A description and explanation of the main outcome measures.* The description and explanation can include information on reliability and validity and samples of the content of the measures.

Box 8.8. How Was Information Collected?

- Standardized reading tests
- Specially developed reading tests
- Interviews with children
- Interviews with parents
- Review of attendance records
- Review of library use

G. *An accounting of the main results,* as in the hypothetical table in Box 8.9. Notice that no decimals are used; numbers should be rounded up to the nearest whole number.

Box 8.9. Ability to Read:
How the Program and the Controls Compare

Age	Program scores	Control scores
4	45	22*
5	46	20*
6	33	29
7	35	32

NOTE: Higher scores are better.
NOTE: *Statistically significant

H. *Conclusions*

Box 8.10. Conclusion

- Younger children benefit more than older children

I. *Alternative explanations, limitations, and problems*

Box 8.11. Do the Results Fit?

- Few comparable program evaluations
- No other competing programs
- Did not evaluate behavior
- No follow-up beyond 1 year

J. *Recommendations*

Box 8.12. Recommendations

- Adopt program for 4- and 5-year-olds
- Revise the program and evaluate again for 6- and 7-year-olds

---

4. *Keep tables and figures simple.* Explain the meaning of the title, the column and row headings, and the statistics. For the table in Box 8.9 above, you can say:

> The next slide compares the knowledge of children in CARP with those in the controls. We used the CARP Test, in which higher scores are better and the highest score is 50 points.
>
> As you can see [if possible, point to the appropriate place on the screen], children who are 4 and 5 years old did significantly better in CARP. We found no differences in children who were 6 and 7 years old.

5. *Check carefully for typographical errors.*

6. *Avoid abbreviations* unless you are certain the listener has been informed and knows what they mean. In the CARP example, its abbreviation was explained in the second visual (see Box 8.4). If necessary, explain and define each acronym.

7. *Outline or write out the talk.*

8. *Rehearse the presentation* before you create the final copies of the visual aids. Then rehearse again. The purpose of the first rehearsal is to make sure the talk is logical, the spelling is correct, and the arrangement of words, figures, and tables is meaningful.

9. *Ensure that visuals are easy to see.* Horizontal placement is better than vertical. It is essential that all potential listeners be able to see the visuals regardless of where they are seated. In advance of the talk, check the room, the seating plan, and the place where you will stand. If you are using slides, hold them up against the light before use. If you cannot see the contents, the audience will not be able to see them either.

10. *Use humor and rhetorical questions to engage listeners.* Typical rhetorical questions are given in three of the visuals above: Who Was in CARP? How Was Information Collected? Do the Results Fit?

EXERCISES: EVALUATION REPORTS

Directions

1. Review the visual aid in Box 8.13. If necessary, improve it.

Box 8.13. Visual Aid #1

A **stratified random sample** is one in which the population is divided into subgroups or "strata," and a random sample is then selected from each group. For example, in a program to teach women about options for combining family, school, and work, the evaluator can sample from a number of subgroups, including women of differing ages (under 19 years, 20 to 30, 31 to 35, over 35) and income (high, medium, low).

Table 8.1. Baseline and Follow-up Mean and Standard Deviation (SD) for
Outcome Variables for HAPPY and Controls (n = 867 Students)

| | *HAPPY* | | *Control* | | | | |
Outcome	*Baseline*	*Follow-Up*	*Baseline*	*Follow-Up*	*Net Difference*	*t*	*p*
Knowledge	75.6 (11.8)	85.5 (8.8)	78.8 (10.9)	81.2 (9.6)	7.5	8.9	.0001
Beliefs	3.5 (0.7)	3.8 (0.7)	3.7 (0.7)	3.8 (0.7)	.19	4.7	.0001
Self-confidence	3.7 (0.7)	3.9 (0.7)	3.7 (0.7)	3.8 (0.7)	.10	2.2	.03
Behavior	1.5 (2.5)	1.3 (2.3)	1.0 (2.0)	1.3(2.4)	−.48	2.8	.006

2. Write the text for Table 8.1.

Suggested Reading

Pfeiffer, W. S. (1991). *Technical writing.* New York: Macmillan.

> Provides useful tips on the details of putting together formal reports.
> Discusses the cover and title page, table of contents, and executive
> summary. Also contains rules for preparing charts and giving oral
> presentations.

Review Notes

Purpose of This Chapter

This chapter focuses on evaluation plans and budgets. An evaluation plan specifies each of the tasks to be accomplished and the personnel, time, and resources needed. For example, if the evaluation is using sampling to identify participants, who will be responsible for drawing up and implementing a sampling plan? By when will the plan be completed? implemented? What resources other than personnel are needed? Is a complete of names available from which to sample? If not, who will get it? How long will that take? Will it cost money?

The chapter addresses issues pertaining to the variety of resources that all evaluations require. Special emphasis is placed on how to determine direct and indirect costs and the relationships between cost and quality. Sample planning and budgeting formats are provided.

9 Evaluation Plans and Budgets

Tasks, Skills, and Resources

An evaluation happens because one or more people are responsible for planning and completing the required tasks. In a very small evaluation, one or two persons may be in charge of all activities. In larger evaluations, teams of individuals with differing skills are involved. Sometimes, evaluations are planned and conducted by the staff with the assistance of consultants who are called in for advice or to complete specific activities.

Planning an evaluation means deciding on the tasks and activities (e.g., monitoring the quality of data collection, implementing a sampling plan) that must be completed. Once the tasks are known, the personnel who have the skills to complete them efficiently can be selected. For example, suppose the evaluation needs to hire someone with experience in drawing samples and overseeing data collection. You may just happen to know someone who needs a job and has both skills. If you do not know the right person, identifying tasks and skills will help you greatly in your job search.

The specific time and financial resources needed for each evaluation will vary according to its size and scope and the number of skills and personnel needed to accomplish each task. Figure 9.1 illustrates the types of skills and resources needed to perform a "typical" evaluation.

Evaluation Task	Skills Needed	Other Resources
Pose Evaluation Questions and Set Standards	Conduct focus groups	• Transportation for participants • Honorariums • Room rental • Refreshments • Materials to guide discussion
	Convene advisors	• Honorariums • Telephone • Mail

Figure 9.1. Typical Evaluation Tasks, Skills, and Resources

Evaluation Task	Skills Needed	Other Resources
	Conduct literature reviews	• Librarian • Reproduction of materials • Expert in abstraction form development • Training expert for reviewers • Space for training
Design the Evaluation	• Know alternative research designs • Implement designs (e.g., identify and assign groups)	• Research design expert • Computer expert • Software • Hardware
Sample Participants	• Have technical expertise in selecting sampling methods, determining sample size, and selecting sample	• Sampling expert • Computer expert • Software • Hardware
Collect Data	• Conduct literature reviews to identify measures • Prepare and assess data collection instruments • Administer and monitor data collection in pilot tests and actual evaluation	See above Expert consultant
Organize the Data	• Code data • Enter data into the computer • Clean data • Prepare codebook	• Programmer • Consultant in data analysis (e.g., what to do with missing data)
Analyze the Data	• Select appropriate data-analytic methods • Perform data analysis	• Programmer • Consultant in data analysis (e.g., statistician and psychometrician)

Figure 9.1. (Continued)

Evaluation Task	Skills Needed	Other Resources
	• Select appropriate psychometric analyses • Conduct appropriate psychometric analyses	• Software • Hardware
Report the Results	• Write report • Disseminate report • Prepare slides or transparencies • Give report orally	• Reproduction and printing • Dissemination (e.g., mail) • Travel to give report orally • Honorariums for reviewers • Editorial consultant • Graphic artist for slides

Figure 9.1. (Continued)

1. POSE EVALUATION QUESTIONS AND SET STANDARDS

A first task requires identifying the evaluation questions and the standards by which program effectiveness will be judged. Focus groups sometimes are used to help in these activities. Effective focus groups require expert leaders. Also, the participants sometimes are remunerated; almost always, they receive refreshments. Other items that might incur costs include renting a meeting room, transportation for the participants, and materials (e.g., pamphlets, survey questionnaires) for participants to use in the group discussion.

An evaluator may decide to convene an advisory group to help in obtaining certification of the educational importance of the evaluation questions and standards of performance. This may require payment of honorariums and result in telephone and mail costs.

To conduct a literature review requires expertise in identifying relevant sources of information from a variety of places (e.g., the library, other public and private agencies), abstracting the information, and displaying the results in a usable fashion. If more than one person is involved in abstracting information, then a standardized form should be prepared so that the same types of information are required from the abstractors. Moreover, the abstractors should be trained to use the form, and the quality of their review should be monitored. Training can take place more than once; depending on the evaluation, anywhere from 1 hour to 2 days may be needed. For example, a 2-day training session is not unusual in large surveys of the literature.

2. DESIGN THE EVALUATION

To design an evaluation requires expertise in research techniques. For example, research knowledge is essential in deciding on the appropriate intervals in longitudinal studies, determining the inclusion and exclusion criteria for the survey, and choosing appropriate and meaningful comparison groups.

3. SAMPLE THE PARTICIPANTS

Sampling usually is considered one of the most technical of all evaluation tasks because knowledge of statistics is essential in deciding on a sample size, choosing and implementing a sampling technique, and determining the adequacy and representativeness of the sample. Large evaluation teams include experts in research design and sampling; smaller evaluations sometimes rely on expert consultation.

Whenever technical activities take place, it is wise to check on the adequacy of the hardware and software available to the survey team. If it is not appropriate, computers or programs may need to be purchased. In some cases, the existing computer facilities are adequate, but special expertise, like programming, is needed so that the special needs of the survey are met.

4. COLLECT THE DATA

If the evaluation plans to use data collection measures adapted from already-existing instruments, expertise is needed in conducting literature reviews to determine whether any instruments are available and potentially useful. It helps to have experience in the subject matter being addressed and to know who is working in the field and might either have instruments or items or know where and how to get them.

Selecting items or rewording them to fit into new instruments requires special skills. The selector must be knowledgeable regarding the evaluation's participants and have experience in assembling items and placing them together.

Preparing an entirely new instrument is daunting. A job description for an instrument writer would call for excellent writing skills and knowledge of the subject matter or topic.

All evaluation measures should be tried out in advance of use; in fact, the entire data collection system should be tested. Pilot testing means having access to a group of potential respondents who are willing to use measures that may be difficult to understand or complete. Expertise is needed in analyzing the data from the pilot, and experience in interpreting respondents' responses is essential.

Pilot testing may be very simple, say a 1-hour tryout in a classroom. In other cases, it may be more complicated, requiring the rental of a room or office and the provision of refreshments. In addition, all measures, even in pilot-test format, must be prepared in a readable, user-friendly format. Assistance from a graphics expert may be useful.

Each evaluation measure has special requirements. Face-to-face and telephone interviews, for example, require skilled personnel. Interviewers must be able to elicit the information called for on the survey instrument and record the answers in the appropriate way. Interviewers must be able to talk with people in a courteous manner and to listen carefully. Also, they must talk and listen efficiently. If the interview is to last, say, no longer than 10 minutes, it must not drag on for 20. Interviews become increasingly costly and even unreliable when they exceed their planned times.

Mailed questionnaires also require skilled personnel. Among the types of expertise required are the ability to prepare a mailing that is user-friendly (e.g., directions are easy to follow, a self-addressed and stamped envelope is included) and the skill to monitor returns and conduct follow-ups with nonrespondents.

Expertise is needed in defining the skills and abilities needed to administer all of the evaluation's data collection activities, and training is key to getting reliable and valid survey data. For example, a poorly trained telephone interviewer is likely to get fewer responses than a well-trained interviewer. Because of the importance of training, many large evaluations use experts in training and education to assist them in designing instructional materials and programs.

In large and long-term evaluations, the quality of data collection must be monitored regularly. Are interviewers continuing to follow instructions? Are completed interviews returned promptly to the evaluation team? If deficiencies are noted, then retraining may be necessary.

Telephone interviews, of course, require telephones. Face-to-face interviews require space for privacy and quiet. Mailed surveys can consume quantities of postage and paper. All types of surveys may include monetary and other incentives to encourage respondents to answer questions. Literature and other record reviews require access to files. Observations may be intrusive. The appropriate permissions must be obtained before using any data collection method. To ensure that the personnel understand and can properly implement confidentiality policies, expert help is often desirable.

5. ORGANIZE THE DATA

Organizing the data means programming, coding, and data entry. Programming requires relatively high-level computer skills. Coding can be very complicated, too, especially if response categories are not precoded and responses are open-ended, requiring coding to take place after the responses are reviewed. Training and computer skills are needed to ensure that data enterers are expert in their tasks. Finally, data cleaning can be a highly skilled task involving decisions regarding what to do about missing data, for example. Expertise often is needed in the preparation of the codebook.

6. ANALYZE THE DATA

Appropriate and justifiable data analysis is dependent on statistical and computer skills. Some evaluations are relatively small and require fairly routine statistical knowledge. Most, however, require comparisons among groups or predictions and explanations of findings. Furthermore, evaluations that rely on surveys of attitudes, values, beliefs, and social and psychological functioning also require knowledge of statistical methods for ascertaining reliability and validity. When data analysis becomes complex, statistical consultation may be advisable.

7. REPORT THE RESULTS

Writing the evaluation report requires communication skills, such as the ability to write and to present results in tables and figures. Oral presentations require skills in public speaking and preparing visual aids such as slides or transparencies. It helps to have outside reviewers critique the report; time must be spent on the critique and any subsequent revisions. Expenses for reports can mount if many are to be printed and disseminated widely.

Time, Scope, and Quality

Evaluators prefer to make their own estimates of the amount of time they need to complete a study. Unfortunately, most evaluations have a due date that must be respected even if the evaluators disagree with it.

The amount of time available for the evaluation is a key factor in its size, scope, quality, and costs. The schedule may limit the evaluator's choice of staff to people who can complete each task within the allotted time. It also places boundaries on the evaluation's design and implementation, may affect quality, and is a determinant of costs. The relationships among the evaluation's schedule, scope, quality, and costs are illustrated in Example 9.1.

Example 9.1. Connections Among Schedule, Scope, Quality, and Costs in Evaluations

The Health Assessment and Prevention Program for Youth (HAPPY) is a school-based, teacher-delivered curriculum to favorably modify health-related knowledge, beliefs, and self-confidence concerning health promotion and disease prevention among an eligible population of high school students from various racial and ethnic backgrounds in a large American city. Standards of program effectiveness consist of sustained modifications in program participants' knowledge, beliefs, behavior, and self-confidence and significant differences between the experimental and control groups.

Boys and girls at or above grade level in reading in the 9th and 11th grades from two pairs of demographically similar high schools were assigned to receive either a special six-lesson health promotion (experimental program) or no formal curriculum (control). Students with poor attendance records were excluded. The 4 schools were selected from the city's 14 academic high schools and were chosen on the basis of their combined representativeness (enrollment size and ethnic composition) of the total population of schools.

Table 9.1 contains an overview of HAPPY's evaluation questions, design, sampling, and measures.

The evaluation team is required to present its findings at the end of 18 months. Accordingly, the following schedule of tasks is prepared.

Table 9.1. An Overview of HAPPY: A Program to Improve Health-Related Behaviors in High School Students

Evaluation Question	How effective is the program in favorably modifying knowledge, beliefs, self-confidence, and behaviors regarding health promotion and disease prevention?
Standard	A statistically and educationally significant improvement over a 3-month period for experimental students
	A statistically and educationally significant difference between experimental and control students
Evaluation Design	An experimental design with concurrent controls and random assignment
Independent Variables	Group participation (experimental and control students)
Strata	Group participation: experimental and control
Inclusion Criteria	Must be in the 9th or 11th grade at the time of study
	Must read English at or above grade level
Exclusion Criteria	Poor attendance (two or more unexcused absences over the last month)
Dependent Variables	Knowledge, beliefs, self-confidence, and behavior
Measures	Knowledge: a 20-item achievement test; beliefs: a 25-item survey; self-confidence: an interview with 22 items; behaviors: a 30-item survey checklist
Criteria for Educational Meaning	Statistically significant findings on both standards. The level of significance was set at $p < .05$.
Sampling Method	A 30% random sample of experimental classes (a cluster) and a 20% random sample of control classes

Schedule of Evaluation Tasks

Months 1 and 2
- Select and assign experimental and control schools and classes
- Prepare instructional and publicity materials to introduce schools to evaluation
- Meet with advisory board to confirm evaluation plans and schedule

Months 3 to 6
- Prepare instruments: achievement test, survey of beliefs, self-confidence interview, behavior checklist
- Review the literature
- Conduct focus groups

Months 7 and 8
- Pilot test instruments
- Revise instruments
- Complete preliminary codebook
- Complete analysis plan

Months 9 and 10
- Train teachers and interviewers
- Administer baseline instruments

Months 11 and 12
- Clean and enter baseline data
- Analyze baseline data
- Complete codebook

Months 12 and 13
- Administer follow-up instruments

Months 14 and 15
- Enter follow-up data
- Analyze all evaluation data

Months 15 and 16
- Write report

Month 17
- Have report reviewed

Month 18
- Complete report
- Disseminate report

Comment

The evaluation team is given 18 months to complete its evaluation. The chief evaluator, sometimes called the "principal investigator" (or "PI," in grants-making language), originally argued for a 2-year evaluation, claiming that the longer time period would produce a better study. The school board, however, said they need information much sooner to justify the continuance (or discontinuance) of the curriculum. Moreover, increasing the duration of the evaluation will necessarily increase its costs in terms of salary and other kinds of support; an increase in the evaluation's budget was rejected.

Here are some of the arguments the PI gave to justify the value of a longer time period for the evaluation:

1. Some of the best staff were not available immediately but could be hired later on. To make employment worthwhile, they needed to be guaranteed at least a year's employment. This could not be assured with the current schedule.
2. All measures must be tailor-made for the evaluation. The relatively short period of time available for instrument development might result in poorer quality instruments than otherwise.
3. A 3-month follow-up is better than no follow-up but not as good as 6 months or even a year. Other evaluations of programs for young people show that good outcomes often diminish after 3 months. The evaluation will not be able to tell anything about the consequences of participation after 3 months.

4. The relatively short follow-up time may be insufficient to validly appraise changes in health-related behaviors among young people.

5. A larger number of schools is preferable. The logistics of selection and assignment require more time than is available. The relatively small number of schools may limit the external validity of the findings.

Evaluation Budgets

How much does an evaluation cost in time and money? This is a two-edged question. A quick answer is the evaluation costs exactly the amount of money and takes exactly the amount of time allocated for it. In terms of money, this can range from $100 to the millions of dollars allocated for national evaluations. In terms of time, evaluations can take 6 months or 10 years (or even more, if they are ongoing).

If you have $10,000 and 1 year to plan and conduct an evaluation, well, that is what you have. The only issue is whether you can conduct an evaluation you believe will have valid findings, given that amount of money. Another answer to the question about the cost of a evaluation is related to an ideal: Given enough time and money, what is the bottom line? As a evaluator, you are likely to encounter both situations. Only experience can tell you whether 10 or 15 days is enough to finish Task X, given the quality of the personnel and other resources (including computer hardware and software, space to work comfortably, etc.) you have available.

In the next example, let's assume that when asked to prepare a budget, you are left to your own devices (common enough in government and foundation funding and in business applications, just to name three situations you may encounter). Being left on your own, however, does not mean that an evaluation can be as expensive as you think it should be; on the contrary, you must be prepared to justify your budget, often in written form. Is 10 days enough of Jones's time, for example? Should the evaluation team be expected to hire a more efficient person, someone who can do Jones's job in less time? To justify Jones's time, you will have to demonstrate that he or she is experienced in the evaluation tasks and definitely likely to complete the task within the time allotted and that the duration of the task is appropriate.

How do you calculate the costs of an evaluation? You cannot prepare a budget without specifying each evaluation activity, when it will be completed, who will be involved in completing each task, how many days each person will spend on each task, the cost per hour or day for each staff person, and other direct costs and indirect costs. Use this checklist to guide you in preparing evaluation budgets.

Determining the Costs of an Evaluation: A Checklist

Learn about direct costs. These are all the expenses you will incur because of the evaluation. These include all salaries and benefits, supplies, travel, and equipment.

Decide on the number of days (or hours) that constitute a working year. Commonly used numbers are 230 (1,840 hours) and 260 days (2,080 hours). Use these numbers to show the proportion of time or "level of effort" given by each staff member.

Example: A person who spends 20% of time on the project (assuming 260 days per year) is spending .20 × 260, or 52 days or 416 hours.

Formulate evaluation tasks or activities in terms of months to complete each.

Example: Prepare the survey instrument during Months 5 and 6.

Estimate the number of days (or hours) you need each person to complete each task.

Example: Jones—10 days; Smith—8 days. If required, convert the days into hours and compute an hourly rate. Example: Jones—10 days or 80 hours.

Learn each person's daily (and hourly) rate.

Example: Jones—$320 per day or $40 per hour; Smith—$200 per day or $25 per hour.

Learn the costs of benefits (e.g., vacation, pension, health)—usually a percentage of salaries. Sometimes benefits are called "labor overhead."

Example: Benefits are 25% of Jones's salary. For example, the cost of benefits for 10 days of Jones's time is 10×320 per day $\times .25$, or $800.

Learn the costs of other expenses that are incurred specifically for this evaluation.

Example: One 2-hour focus group with 10 participants costs $650. Each participant gets $25 honorarium, for a total of $250; refreshments cost $50; a focus group expert facilitator costs $300; the materials costs $50 for reproduction, notebooks, name tags, etc.

Learn the *indirect costs,* or the costs that are incurred to keep the evaluation team going. Every individual and institution has indirect costs, sometimes called "overhead" or "general and administrative costs" (G and A). Indirect costs are sometimes a prescribed percentage of the total costs of the evaluation (e.g., 10%).

Example: All routine costs of doing "business," such as workers' compensation and other insurance; attorney's and license fees; lights, rent, and supplies such as paper and computer disks.

If the evaluation lasts more than 1 year, build in cost-of-living increases.

In for-profit consultation and contracting, you may be able to include a "fee." The fee is usually a percentage of the entire cost of the project and may range from about 3% to 10%.

Be prepared to justify all costs in writing.

Example: The purchases included in the budget are 2,000 labels (2 per student interviewed) for use by site staff; envelopes; and $486 for one copy of MIRACLE software for the data management program.

DIRECT COSTS

Salaries, Evaluation Tasks, Months to Complete,
and Number of Days for Each Task

The evaluation team is asked to prepare an 18-month budget for HAPPY (Example 9.1). The team consists of four people: (a) Ingrid Miller, Ed.D., is the principal investigator. She has conducted many evaluations and is an expert in health education. (b) Paul Rubenstein, Ph.D., has interest and experience in adolescent health measurement. (c) Roberta Hays, Ph.D., is a statistician who is also a capable psychometrician. (d) Marvin Oishi, M.Ed., is the project director; his responsibilities will include coordinating the data collection at the schools. Consultants will be hired to prepare publicity and instructional materials, conduct focus groups, train teachers to administer tests and other measures, and conduct interviews with students. An advisory committee of six people (two teachers, two parents, and two students) will be called on for assistance.

The evaluation team begins the budget preparation process by drafting a chart that contains a description of the tasks to be accomplished, the months during which the tasks will be performed and completed, and the total number of days that staff will need to complete each task. This is illustrated in Figure 9.2.

This chart enables the evaluation team to tell how long each task will take and how much staff time will be used. For example, 140 days of staff time are needed to prepare the final report. Obviously, many days of staff time cost more than fewer days.

Preparing a chart like this is essential. First, it helps you decide where you may need to trim the budget because you can ask questions like: Why do Hays and Rubenstein need a total of 30 days to revise the final report? What is Oishi's role in preparing the final report? The chart is also useful because it tells how much time each person will be needed for the particular project.

Task	Months	Staff	Number of Days Spent on-Task	Total
Select and assign experimental and control schools and classes	1-2	Miller Hays Oishi	30 30 30	90
Prepare instructional and publicity materials	1-2	Miller Oishi	5 5	10
Meet with advisors	1-2	Miller Hays Rubenstein Oishi	1 1 1 1	4
Prepare instruments (including literature review and focus groups)	3-6	Miller Hays Rubenstein Oishi	40 30 30 40	140
Pilot and revise the instrument	7-8	Miller Hays Rubenstein Oishi	20 20 30 20	90
Complete analysis plan and preliminary codebook	7-8	Miller Hays Oishi	10 20 20	50
Train teachers and interviewers	9-10	Miller Rubenstein	15 5	20
Administer baseline instruments	9-10	Miller Oishi	20 40	60
Enter and clean data; prepare codebook	11-12	Hays Oishi Miller	40 20 10	70
Administer follow-up instruments	12-13	Miller Oishi	20 40	60

continued

Figure 9.2. Tasks, Months, and Staff Days

Task	Months	Staff	Number of Days Spent on-Task	Total
Enter and analyze data	14-15	Hays Oishi Miller	40 20 30	90
Write report and have it reviewed	15-17	Miller Hays Rubenstein Oishi	30 20 20 5	75
Prepare final report	18	Miller Hays Rubenstein Oishi	30 15 15 5	65

Figure 9.2. (Continued)

Resources and Additional Resources

Practically all evaluations require secretarial and clerical support. These persons may receive benefits, in addition to salary, if they are employed for a certain percentage of time (percentage may vary). Secretarial and clerical support are considered direct costs.

You also need to identify any special resources needed for this particular evaluation activity. Figure 9.3 contains a list of additional resources that potentially are needed in the evaluation.

Budgets can be prepared for specific activities, for individual staff, and for the entire survey. In Example 9.2, the contents of a budget are illustrated for the evaluation of HAPPY. The associated monetary figures are not included because they vary so much from place to place and over time that information presented at this time may appear ridiculous later on. It may be helpful to point out that, in 1994, the bottom line for an evaluation of a program like HAPPY (with its relatively complex sampling scheme, control groups, and multiple measures) cost more than $500,000. An evaluation should

Task	Special Resources
Prepare instructional and publicity materials to introduce schools and teachers to the evaluation	Publicity consultant; materials (notebooks, materials, etc.)
Implement selection and assignment of schools and classes	Honorariums to participating schools for assistance with additional burdens on clerical staff
Conduct focus groups	Honorariums for participants; refreshments; notebooks for participants' materials
Review literature	Reproduction of articles and instruments; research assistant to abstract all studies in a standardized manner
Prepare instruments	Graphics specialist to help format the instruments; special software for the graphics
Pilot-test instruments	Honorariums for pilot test participants and sites
Train teachers and interviewers	Experts in training; interviewers who can talk with young people about health habits
Enter the data	Trained data enterers
Analyze the data	Programmer
Prepare the report	Paper for multiple copies of the report; graphic specialist for tables; program for setting up slides, slide-preparation expert to prepare them for use

Figure 9.3. Additional Resources

comprise about 10% to 20% of a program's budget. Also, Example 9.2 uses a general format for recording budgetary information. All funding agencies have specific budget formats. If you have all the needed information, you will not have trouble translating from one format to another.

Example 9.2. Contents of a Budget for Activities, Staff, and the Entire Evaluation

1. Budget Contents for an Activity: Prepare Instruments

Direct Costs	Cost ($)	Total
Personnel		
Miller		
40 days		
Hays		
30 days		
Rubenstein		
30 days		
Oishi		
40 days		
Secretarial support		
40 days		

Personnel Subtotal

Benefits (or labor overhead; a percentage of the subtotal)

Benefits Subtotal

Other Direct Costs

Consultant

Graphics expert

Purchases

MIRACLE software

Other Direct Costs Subtotal

Indirect Costs

10% of direct costs

TOTAL BUDGET FOR TASK

---

2. Budget Contents for Staff: Ingrid Miller

Direct Costs	Cost ($)	Total
Days spent on evaluation: 301		
Salary per day		
TOTAL		

---

3. Total Budget: 18 Months

Direct costs	Cost ($)	Total

*Personnel**

Miller

261 days

Rubenstein

101 days

Hays

216 days

Oishi

246 days

Secretarial support

390 days

Personnel Subtotal

Benefits (a percentage of the subtotal)

Miller

Rubenstein

Hays

Oishi

Secretary (Garcia)

Benefits Subtotal

Other Direct Costs

Consultants

Private and Public Publicity, Inc.
Lanita Chow, Slide preparation
Graphics artist: To be named
ABC Data Entry, Inc.
John Becke, Programmer
Institute for Interview Training
2 Level A research assistants
10 interviewers

Purchases

MIRACLE software
Paper

Other Direct Costs

Reproduction of reports, instruments, and forms
Honorariums
Printing

Other Direct Costs Subtotal

Indirect Costs

10% of direct costs

TOTAL BUDGET FOR TASK

NOTE: *Month 1 is assumed to be July. In Month 13 (August), all salaries will be increased by 5% to reflect a cost-of-living rise.

Budget Justification

Budgets often are accompanied by a justification of any or all of the following: choice of personnel, amount of time they are to spend on a task or on the project, salaries, other direct costs, indirect costs, and any fees or purchases of equipment and supplies. Example 9.3 illustrates how to present budget justifications for staff, focus groups, and purchase of software.

Example 9.3. Budget Justification

Personnel

Ingrid Miller is the principal investigator. She will spend 261 days (or 77%) of her professional time on the project. Dr. Miller has conducted local and national health education evaluations, the most recent of which is The B-Elementary School Behavior Health Assessment and Prevention Program (Be-HAPPY). For Be-HAPPY, she successfully performed all of the tasks required in the present study, including research design and sampling, instrument preparation, the conduct of literature reviews and focus groups, survey design, data analysis, and report writing. Dr. Miller has worked as a evaluator in this institution for 10 years. Her salary is based on her experience and education and is consistent with the salary schedule described in our institutional handbook (which is on file).

Focus Groups

Focus groups will be conducted to assist in determining the objectives of the survey. We plan to have six participants including two students, two parents, and two teachers. Each will receive an honorarium of $XX for a total of $XXX. Each participant will receive a specially designed notebook with materials for discussion. Each notebook is $X, and 10 will cost $XX. Light refreshments include cookies and soft drinks at $X per person, for a total of $XX.

Software

MIRACLE is a multipurpose graphics program that permits camera-ready instrument preparation. Comparison shopping (estimates upon request) found the least expensive price to be $486.

HOW TO REDUCE COSTS

One of the most difficult aspects of budget preparation usually is performed after the bottom line—the total—is calculated. The reason is that during the first try, the evaluators include everything they think they need, and probably then some. Invariably, the budget needs trimming. The following are recommended ways to reduce the costs of an evaluation.

Guidelines for Reducing Evaluation Costs

♦ Cut down on the scope of the evaluation. Here is where to consider cutting:

Ask fewer evaluation questions.

Simplify standards (e.g., use historical or normed data, rather than data from a comparison group, for some outcomes).

Shorten the duration of the evaluation.

Keep the number of interim reports to a minimum.

Limit pilot testing of new instruments to nine or fewer respondents. (If you pilot on 10 or more, you may need to get "clearance." Nine or fewer in your pilot test saves time and money.)

♦ Shorten instrument preparation time by adapting items and ideas from other measures.

♦ Keep survey instruments short to reduce interviewer and respondent time.

♦ Use nonfinancial incentives for participation, such as certificates of appreciation.

♦ Use less expensive staff for day-to-day activities.

♦ Save expensive staff for consultation and leadership.

♦ Comparison shop for all supplies and equipment.

♦ Reduce the comprehensiveness of some activities (e.g., Do you really need an exhaustive literature review, or will a selective one suffice?)

♦ Shorten the amount of time each evaluation activity takes.

♦ Use transparencies, rather than slides, for oral presentations.

♦ Keep the written report as short as possible.

♦ Share dissemination expenses (e.g., reproduction, mailing) with others.

EXERCISE FOR EVALUATION PLANS AND BUDGETS

Suppose an evaluation team has been asked to evaluate a computer science and mathematics program for elementary school children. The evaluators are to survey children each year for 5 years. The survey is to be a mailed, self-administered questionnaire.

The evaluation team has been asked to plan and prepare a budget for the first year's survey. They have prepared two documents: *Task, Months, and Staff Days,* and *Tasks and Special Resources.* The team consists of Marvin Lee, Yuki Smith, and Beth Jones.

Directions

Using Documents 1 and 2, outline the contents of a budget, showing the costs of:

1. the task: Prepare Report Orally
2. personnel: Marvin Lee
3. total costs of the survey for the year

Document 1: Tasks, Months, and Staff Days

Task	Months	Staff	Number of Days Spent on-Task	Total
Identify survey objectives: Conduct literature review	1	Smith Jones Lee	20 10 5	35
Identify survey objectives and standards: organize and conduct focus groups	1	Jones Lee	10 5	15
Design the survey	2	Lee Smith	15 5	20
Prepare the survey	3	Lee Jones Smith	20 15 15	50
Pilot the instrument	4	Lee Smith Jones	15 10 10	35
Revise the instrument	5	Lee Smith	10 5	15
Administer the survey	6	Lee Smith	10 10	20
Enter and clean data; prepare code book	7	Lee Smith Jones	10 3 15	28
Analyze the data	8	Lee Jones	15 15	30
Write the report	9	Lee Smith Jones	15 5 5	25

Task	Months	Staff	Number of Days Spent on-Task	Total
Have the report reviewed	10	Lee	5	5
Revise the report	11	Lee	10	10
Prepare final report and oral presentation:		Lee Smith Jones	15 10 10	35
Written report	12			
Oral presentation		Lee Smith Jones	5 5 5	15

Document 2: Tasks and Special Resources

Task	Special resources
Review literature	Reproduction of reports and surveys; reproduction of forms for abstracting content of literature
Conduct focus groups	Honorariums for participants; refreshments; notebooks for participants' materials
Design the survey	Honorariums for clerical staff for assistance in reviewing addresses
Prepare the survey instrument	Graphics specialist to help format the questionnaire
Administer the survey	Postage for one original and one follow-up mailing; printing costs for questionnaire
Enter the data	Trained data enterer
Analyze the data	Programmer, statistical consultation
Prepare the report	Paper for multiple copies of the report; graphic specialist for tables
Give the report orally	Program for setting up slides; slide-preparation expert to prepare them for use

Answers to Exercises

CHAPTER 1

1. The evaluation questions are:

   ♦ To what extent do participants demonstrate key competencies?

   ♦ How enduring are the effects? (e.g., Are they sustained 1 year after completion of the program? 2 years?)

   ♦ For which types of trainees is the program most effective (e.g., younger and older trainees; trainees with more and less experience)?

2. The standards are favorable comparison with previous trainees (e.g., more versatile and knowledgeable), measures of the adequacy of student performance, and sustained improvement (implicit in the evaluation because trainees will be followed from entry into the program until 2 years after graduation).

3. The design is historical comparisons with previous trainees and self-comparisons over times (at entry and 1 and 2 years later).

4. Data collection measures being used are tests, surveys, observations, and student performance data.

5. Additional information needed to perform the evaluation are:

- An explicit statement of the standards. For example, if changes are observed in versatility of teaching methods and knowledge, how will the adequacy of those changes be assessed?
- An explanation and justification of the numbers and types of individuals who will participate in the evaluation. For example, will all trainees be included? Are the samples large enough to discern true differences?
- A description of the number of observations and when they will be made
- The data-analytic methods

CHAPTER 2

1. Evaluation questions
   a.. Have teachers learned the guidelines for selecting textbooks?
   b. How accurate and up-to-date are the textbooks?
   c. Have all grades benefited equally?
2. *Question:* Did personnel become knowledgeable about privacy issues pertaining to student participation in experimental programs?
   Standards:
   - Eighty percent of personnel become knowledgeable about privacy issues.
   - An improvement in knowledge is observed before and after the program (for up to 5 years).
   - A difference in knowledge is found between current and future personnel.

   Independent variable: Personnel
   Dependent variable: Knowledge

CHAPTER 3

Evaluation Question 1: Has the center's education improved?
Standard: Reading ability improves over the 2-year program period.
Independent variable: Participation in the program
Design: An experimental evaluation with self-controls

Potential biases: During the 2-year period, a number of external events having nothing to do with the program may influence practice. For example, the World Health Organization or a charitable foundation might provide additional or new funds for education, or refugees may move on or drop out of the program. A control group can guard against the influence of outside variables.

Evaluation Question 2: How satisfied are participating refugees and teachers with the quality of education?

Standard: No judgment can be made regarding the answers to this question because it is solely for descriptive information.

Design: Survey

Potential biases: This design will provide a cross section of opinions. It cannot produce data on the extent to which the views of the responding individuals have been affected by the program or how the views compare with those held by nonparticipants.

CHAPTER 4

1. C
2. B
3. A

CHAPTER 5

1. E
2. A
3. D
4. B
5. C

CHAPTER 6

1. A. *Content validity* because the instrument is based on a number of theoretical constructs (e.g., the health beliefs model and social learning theory).

B. *Interrater reliability* because agreement is correlated between scorers. If we also assume that each expert's ratings are true, then we have concurrent validity. Kappa (κ) is a statistic used to adjust for agreements that could have arisen by chance alone.

C. *Test-retest reliability* because each test is scored twice.

2. a. Example of a form, with coding strip, to determine student's ability to get to school on time (see Box A.1)

Box A.1

In the past 2 weeks, has this student arrived at school on time?
(Mark *one* choice)

Always arrives on time	1	*1*
Has been late one or two times	2	
Has been late three or four times	3	
Is almost always late	4	
No opportunity to observe	9	

---

b. Example of a form, with coding strip, to determine whether the student manages time appropriately (see Box A.2)

Box A.2

In the past 4 weeks, how often did this student complete all school-related tasks?
(Mark *one* choice)

Always	1	*2*
Usually	2	
Sometimes	3	
Rarely	4	
No opportunity to observe	9	

---

c. Example of a form, with coding strip, to determine whether the student maintains satisfactory relationships with other students and teachers (see Box A.3)

During the past 4 weeks, how satisfactory has this student's relationship been with teachers and other students? Use this scale:

5 = Extremely satisfactory

4 = Satisfactory

3 = Between satisfactory and unsatisfactory

2 = Unsatisfactory

1 = Extremely unsatisfactory

9 = No opportunity to observe

Box A.3

Choose *one*.

Teachers	5	4	3	2	1	9	3
Other students	5	4	3	2	1	9	

---

3. This information collection plan has several serious flaws. First, it only anticipates collecting data on student knowledge and skill despite the fact that the objectives also pay attention to attitude. Second, even if the evaluators are expert test constructors, they must pilot test and evaluate the tests to determine their reliability and validity. Third, the evaluators do not plan to monitor the use of the educational materials. If faculty cannot or will not use them, then any results may be spurious. The 5-year plan of testing is, however, probably of sufficient duration to observe changes.

CHAPTER 7

1.

Situation	Describe Independent and Dependent Variables	Tell Whether the Data Are Nominal, Ordinal, or Numerical
Children in the experimental and control groups are tested to determine whether their reading ability improved, remained the same, or worsened.	Independent variable: group; dependent variable: reading ability	Independent variable is nominal; dependent variable is ordinal.
Participants in the program are grouped according to whether they are severely, moderately, or marginally depressed and are given a survey of anxiety that is scored from 1 to 9.	Independent variable: depressed patients in the program; dependent variable: anxiety	Independent variable is ordinal; dependent variable is numerical.
Children are chosen for the evaluation according to whether they have had all recommended vaccinations or not; they are followed for 5 years.	Independent variable: having or not having recommended vaccinations; dependent variable: health status	Independent variable is nominal; not enough information to tell about the dependent variable.
Boys and girls from higher and lower income families are compared in the quality of their lives as measured by scores ranging from 1 to 50 that are obtained from standardized observations.	Independent variables: gender and income; dependent variable: quality of life	Independent variables are nominal and ordinal; dependent variable is numerical.

Situation	Describe Independent and Dependent Variables	Tell Whether the Data Are Nominal, Ordinal, or Numerical
Instructors and supervisors are surveyed, and their average scores are compared.	Independent variables: personnel (supervisors and instructors); dependent variable: proficiency	Independent variable is nominal; dependent variable is numerical.

2. Analysis: A two-sample independent groups *t* test
   Justification for the analysis: This *t* test is appropriate when the independent variable is measured on a nominal scale and the dependent variable is measured on a numerical scale. In this case, the assumptions of a *t* test are met. These assumptions are (a) each group has a sample size of at least 30, (b) the sizes of the groups are about equal, and (c) the two groups are independent (an assumption that is met most easily with a strong evaluation design and a high-quality data collection effort).

3. If the evaluation aims to determine how younger and older persons in the experimental and control group compare in amount of domestic violence, and presuming that the statistical assumptions are met, then an analysis of variance is an appropriate technique.

CHAPTER 8

1. Box 8.13 requires that the audience read too much. Also, the title of a visual should be more informative. The text suggests two visuals, presented in Boxes A.4 and A.5.

Box A.4. Stratified Random Sampling

Population is divided into subgroups or strata
Random sample is selected from each stratum

Box A.5. Stratified Random Sampling: Blueprint

Income	*Age, y*			
	Under 19	*20-30*	*31-35*	*Over 35*
High				
Medium				
Low				

2. Sample text for the table: The table presents the baseline and follow-up means and the observed net change scores for each of four main outcomes for 867 HAPPY and control students. Significant outcomes for HAPPY were knowledge, beliefs, and behavior.

CHAPTER 9

Outline of the Contents of a Budget for Activities, Staff, and the Entire Survey

This is a budget for a 1-year, mailed questionnaire.

1. Budget Contents for an Activity: Give Report Orally

Direct Costs	Cost ($)	Total

Survey Personnel

Marvin Lee

    15 days

Beth Jones

    10 days

Yuki Smith

    10 days

Secretarial support

    15 days

Direct Costs   Cost ($)   Total

Personnel Subtotal

Benefits (a percentage of the subtotal)
  Marvin Lee
  Beth Jones
  Yuki Smith

Benefits subtotal

Other Direct Costs

Consultant
  Slide preparation

Purchases
  MIRACLE software

Other Direct Costs Subtotal

Indirect Costs
  10% of direct costs
  TOTAL BUDGET FOR TASK

2. Budget Contents for Staff: Marvin Lee

Direct costs

  Days spent on survey: 155
  Salary per day
  Benefits

Indirect costs

  TOTAL FOR MARVIN LEE

Direct Costs   Cost ($)   Total

3. Total Budget for Year

Survey Personnel

    Marvin Lee

        155 days

    Beth Jones

        95 days

    Yuki Smith

        88 days

    Secretarial support

        165 days

Personnel subtotal

Benefits (a percentage of the subtotal)

    Marvin Lee

    Beth Jones

    Yuki Smith

Benefits Subtotal

Other Direct Costs

Consultants

    Lanita Chow, Slide preparation

    Graphics artist: To be named

    ABC Data Entry, Inc.

    John Becke, Programmer

    Eduard Parker, Statistician

Purchases

    MIRACLE software

    Paper

Direct Costs	Cost ($)	Total

Other Direct Costs

    Reproduction of reports, surveys, and forms
    Honorariums
    Postage for survey mailings
    Printing

Other Direct Costs Subtotal

Indirect Costs

    10% of direct costs
    TOTAL BUDGET

Index

About the Author

ARLENE FINK, Ph.D., is a Professor of Medicine and Public Health at the University of California, Los Angeles. She is on the Research Advisory Board of UCLA's Robert Wood Johnson Clinical Scholars Program; a health research scientist at the Veterans Administration Medical Center, Sepulveda, CA; and President of Arlene Fink Associates. She has conducted evaluations throughout the United States and abroad and has trained thousands of health professionals, social scientists, and educators in program evaluation. In addition, she has published nearly 100 monographs and articles connected with evaluation methods and research. She is the coauthor of *How to Conduct Surveys* and the author of *Evaluation Fundamentals: Guiding Health Programs, Research, and Policy.*